KwaZulu-Natal

ADVENTURES IN CULTURE & NATURE

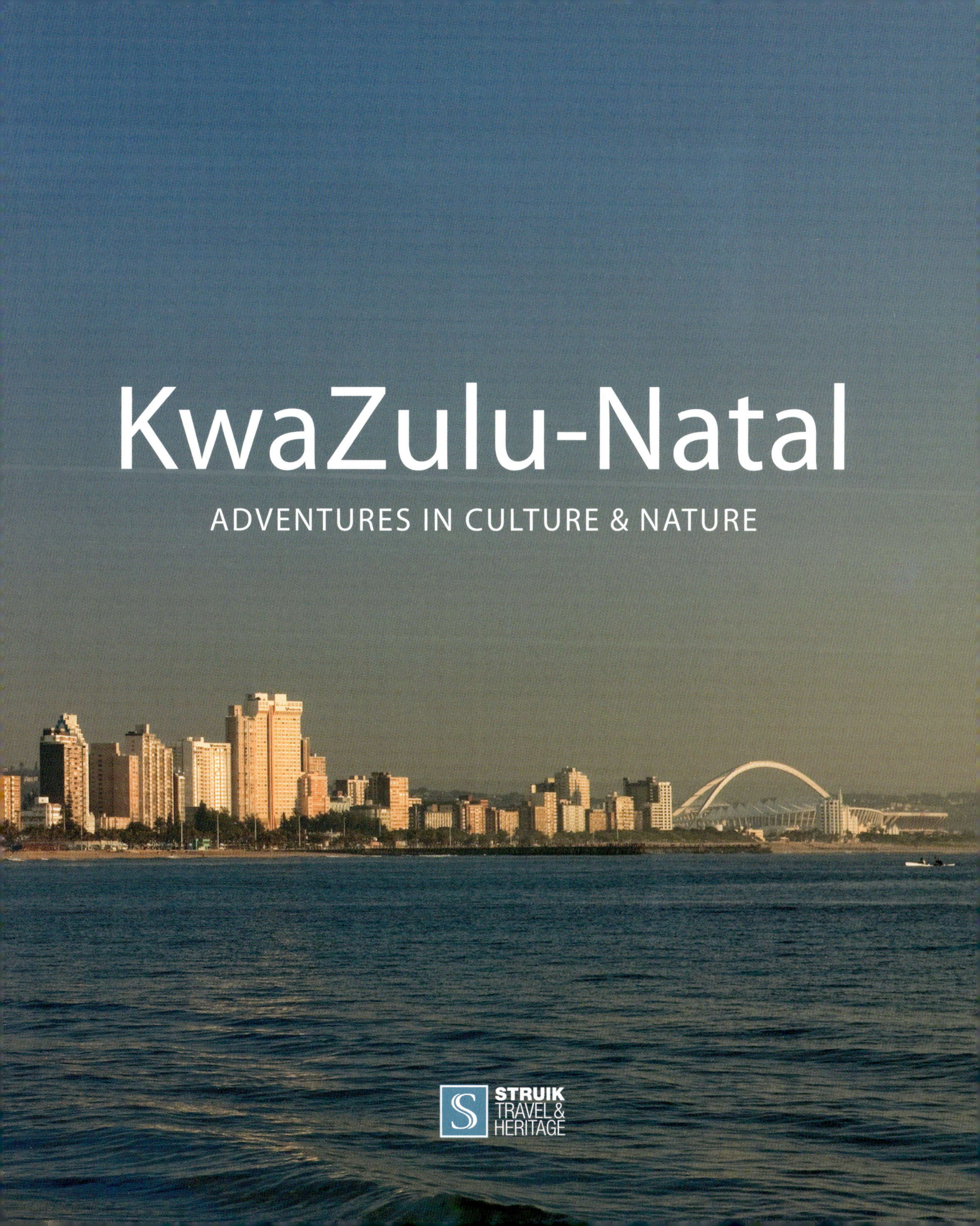

KwaZulu-Natal

ADVENTURES IN CULTURE & NATURE

STRUIK TRAVEL & HERITAGE

CONTENTS

Author's note — 6

1 Introduction — 8
   ■ Welcome to KZN ■ KZN Fact File

2 The People — 12
   ■ San ■ Zulus ■ Indians ■ Europeans

3 Faiths of the People — 24
   ■ Shembe ■ Muslims ■ Jews ■ Christians
   ■ Hindus ■ Buddhists

4 Creative Thinking — 38
   ■ Architecture ■ Visual arts ■ Performing arts

5 Playing Games — 50
   ■ Races and events ■ Adventure sports

6 Food and Drink — 60
   ■ Good fare ■ Alcohol

7 Beach and Sea — 72
■ Beaches ■ Activities ■ Marine environment

8 Game and Nature Parks — 86
■ Managing the wilds ■ Conservation efforts
■ Ezemvelo KZN Wildlife's major reserves
■ Private game reserves ■ Nature reserves and conservancies ■ Taming the wilds

9 World Heritage Wetland — 100
■ iSimangaliso Wetland Park ■ Transfrontier conservation areas ■ History and conservation
■ Cultural tourism ■ Places to stay ■ Things to do

10 World Heritage Mountains — 116
■ uKhahlamba-Drakensberg Park ■ Rock art
■ Places to stay ■ Things to do

Contact details — 134

Index — 140

AUTHOR'S NOTE

AUTHOR'S NOTE

I have lived in the beautiful South African province of KwaZulu-Natal most of my life, and even though I have been fortunate to travel quite extensively, to other provinces and distant shores, I have never wanted to reside anywhere else. After all, this is the place where nearly everyone else in the country aspires to come during their time off.

For those of us who live here, it is so easy to feel as if we are permanently on holiday. It is a great place to kick back and relax, to unwind and rejuvenate the soul. Who would want to be anywhere else?

I love that the sea is warm, the sun is hot, the leaves are big and sultry. That there is snow on the mountains and there are whales in the sea, and that the people are laid-back and friendly. I love that it is one of the few places left in the world where strong, living, traditional cultures still impact directly and daily on modern people's lives.

For visitors and residents alike, I write about this beautiful province on the east coast of Africa to provide some information about some of the places to visit as well as, hopefully, to inspire readers to step outside and discover more about the environment and themselves.

By all accounts, once you have been here, you will definitely want to visit again – and like me, you may not want to leave!

Sue Derwent
Durban 2010

BELOW: *The warm Indian Ocean washes up on the protected beaches of Durban's bay.*

1

INTRODUCTION

Land of brave Zulu warriors and artistic San, rolling battlefields and colonial outposts, rich, protected wetlands and the awe-inspiring Drakensberg Mountains, mission churches, temples and mosques – KwaZulu-Natal simply exudes history, natural beauty and culture.

INTRODUCTION

PREVIOUS PAGE: *Surrounded by giant sycamore and luminescent lime-green fever trees, Ndumo's pans draw large numbers of water birds, as well as hippo and crocodile.*

BELOW: *The Buffalo River, seen here near Fugitives Drift, winds past and through several historic battle sites, which look much the same as they did during the conflict.*

WELCOME TO KZN

The magnificent province of KwaZulu-Natal is often known simply as KZN. It is generally divided into eight regions, namely Durban, the South Coast, the North Coast, Pietermaritzburg and Midlands, the Battlefields, uKhahlamba-Drakensberg, Zululand and the Maputaland. Each of these areas has its own unique characteristics and attractions, and visitors will find they are quite spoilt for choice.

With the seemingly perpetual summer of its subtropical climate it is a holiday-maker's delight, where average temperatures vary between 28 °C in summer and just 23 °C in winter. Not surprisingly, KZN is famous for its outdoor activities, beaches, nature-based tourism facilities, sporting events and the variety of its adventure activities. For instance, adrenaline junkies can get their fix by abseiling the world's highest gorge, diving among ragged-tooth sharks, ice climbing, whitewater rafting or mountain biking.

Some of South Africa's top game reserves are situated in KZN and conservation tourism is highly developed. Two such parks are World Heritage Sites, namely iSimangaliso Wetland Park and uKhahlamba-Drakensberg Park. Also in KZN is the publicly owned, celebrated Hluhluwe-iMfolozi Park, which is famous for its white rhino populations. Privately owned game reserves also offer a range of game-viewing facilities and accommodation to suit all pockets and preferences.

Politically and historically, the battles fought in the beautiful hills and valleys of northern KZN at the end of the 19th century changed the course of

South African history. The sites of famous skirmishes that rocked the British, weakened the Boers and broke the mighty Zulu nation continue to draw visitors. Some of the more famous of the numerous battlefields are Rorke's Drift and Isandlwana, but there are also fascinating historical sites, museums and monuments throughout the province.

The diversity of cultures is apparent in the many museums, churches, temples and mosques, as well as in the music, architecture, theatre, dance and art. Food is a joy, and many exciting local culinary delights await exploration.

Durban, KZN's largest city, is also home to the leading traditional healers' market in the Southern Hemisphere. Indeed, no matter what your interests, there really is something for everyone in KZN.

KZN FACT FILE

Name	*KwaZulu* means 'place of the Zulu people'. *eZulweni*, from which the name 'Zulu' is derived, means 'heaven' or 'sky above'. The name 'Natal' dates back to 1497, when Portuguese explorer Vasco da Gama sighted the coastline on Christmas day, naming it *Terra de Natalia* in reference to the birth of Christ. The two names were joined after the 1994 elections to form KwaZulu-Natal, often referred to as KZN by South Africans.
Location	The province of KZN sits on South Africa's eastern seaboard, bounded by the Indian Ocean.
Neighbouring countries and provinces	Mozambique, Swaziland, Lesotho, Mpumalanga, Free State and Eastern Cape.
Municipalities	KZN has 11 districts, as follows: Amajuba (Newcastle) Zululand (Ulundi) Umkhanyakude (Mkuze) uThungulu (Richards Bay) Umzinyathi (Dundee) Uthukela (Ladysmith) Umgungundlovu (Pietermaritzburg) iLembe (kwaDukuza, formerly Stanger) eThekwini (Durban) Ugu (Port Shepstone) Sisonke (Ixopo)
Capital city	Pietermaritzburg
Major cities and towns	Durban, Pietermaritzburg, Port Shepstone, Margate, Richards Bay, Ulundi
Protected areas	There is a system of approximately 96 protected areas covering some 8% of the province. The larger parks include Hluhluwe-iMfolozi Park, iSimangaliso Wetland Park and uKhahlamba-Drakensberg Park.
Area	92 060 km²
Share of total area of South Africa	7,7%
Coastline	599,73 km
Population	10 449 300 (mid-2009 estimate)
Population density	113 people per km²
Home language	80,9% Zulu, 13,6% English, 2,3% Xhosa, 1,5% Afrikaans, 1,7% other
Climate	Subtropical
Average summer temperatures	Durban 21–28 °C, Pietermaritzburg 18–28 °C, Richards Bay 21–29 °C
Average winter temperatures	Durban 11–23 °C, Pietermaritzburg 3–23 °C, Richards Bay 12–23 °C
Average annual rainfall	919 mm

Sources: Chief Directorate: Surveys and Mapping, Ezemvelo KZN Wildlife, South African Weather Service and Statistics SA

2

THE PEOPLE

One of the best ways to get to know an area is by understanding the culture and history of the locals. KZN is filled with a friendly, fascinating diversity of people who have helped make the province the vibrant, interesting region that it is, filled with complex contradictions.

PREVIOUS PAGE: *Elegant and colourful Hindu temple dancers are a delight to watch.*

ABOVE AND OPPOSITE: *The Game Pass Shelter in the Kamberg area of uKhahlamba-Drakensberg Park is one of the finest places to view San rock art.*

SAN

There is evidence of San habitation throughout the province. The Drakensberg San were small groups of hunter-gatherers who lived in the caves and rock shelters of these mountains. It is here, on the rock faces, that their amazing paintings, dating back some 8 000 years, can be found. This fabulous legacy of rock art, considered to be some of the best in the world, is the most extensive in Africa.

Four major groupings of San and some smaller clans once lived in the Drakensberg region. The Baroa were found in and around Lesotho, the !Ga!Nē in the Transkei area near Tsolo/Maclear, the //Xegwi in the Central Drakensberg (their descendants can now be found living near Ermelo), and the Ku//e lived near the Free State border with Lesotho. There was also a smaller group, the Thola from the Griqualand East region, who were known to be horse riders.

As the San were thought to be extinct in this region, myths developed around their rock art, shamans, rainmaking abilities and healing skills. Interestingly, recent sociological and anthropological research has revealed that they are not in fact extinct (see box p. 15). In addition, their connection to the environment and spirit world is well documented.

Experiencing San culture

Guided walks to rock shelters and caves at **Injisuthi**, **Giant's Castle**, **Kamberg**, **Cathedral Peak** and the **Royal Natal Park** can be booked through Ezemvelo KZN Wildlife or AMAFA (see World Heritage Mountains pp. 125 & 131–32).

THE PEOPLE

ZULUS

The Nguni people, to whom the amaZulu belong, began to arrive in the region from north and east Africa some time during the 17th century. They emerged as a regional power in the early 1800s under the legendary Zulu King Shaka, and by 1879 the Zulu armies, led by Cetshwayo, were sufficiently strong and organised to inflict a massive defeat upon the British at the battle of Isandlwana. To date, it is the worst defeat the British have ever suffered against an indigenous army.

However, although the Zulus continued to fight valiantly for their land against both Boer and British, they were finally defeated in 1879 at the battle of uLundi. Their kingdom was broken up and formally incorporated into British Natal as the century came to a close.

Over the years, Zulu speakers have been dispersed throughout the country, firstly in the mass migrations that took place during King Shaka's reign and later during the apartheid years, when the migrant labour system saw thousands of rural Zulu men leave their homes to work on the mines on the Witwatersrand.

Experiencing Zulu culture

Some people feel that visiting **cultural villages** is an inauthentic or commercial undertaking, however

The secret San

While working in the Drakensberg foothills, anthropologist Frans Prins heard about people who described themselves as descendants of *abaThwa* – the Bushmen clans.

For generations descendants of the Drakensberg San had not felt free to identify themselves for fear of discrimination and intimidation. This is not surprising, considering their history.

The San were victimised by whites, blacks and farmers. Many were killed while others moved away or became assimilated into black society, where they were often treated with suspicion and hostility.

Today, because of their perceived mastery of the elements and connections to the spirit world, some San descendants have ritual status in their communities as rainmakers or healers. However, the moment anything goes wrong, the same individuals are likely to be blamed. Happily things are slowly changing for the better, and with support some descendants of the Drakensberg San are beginning to reclaim their heritage.

THE PEOPLE

these are the best places to get a solid background on Zulu traditions and culture. Insightful for adults, a stopoff is also educational and great fun for children. Most cultural villages offer tours that show the traditional homes and their arrangement, explain the role of cattle and allow visitors to see traditional crafters at work. Visitors can also meet a traditional healer, called a sangoma, and enjoy home-made sorghum beer and a delicious local meal. A visit usually ends with some festive, foot-stomping Zulu dancing.

Shakaland was originally built as part of the set of the internationally acclaimed film, *Shaka Zulu*, and as such it is one of the better-known cultural villages. Part of the set was transformed into accommodation, allowing visitors to stay overnight. Spear-throwing demonstrations are a highlight, after which visitors get an opportunity to test their skills.

DumaZulu Lodge & Traditional Village has been kept as authentic as possible. Each unit of the overnight accommodation is designed to represent a different African cultural group, in keeping with their traditional architectural styles. Adjacent to the village is a snake and crocodile park.

PheZulu Safari Park, just 20 minutes outside of Durban, is an easily accessible, albeit somewhat more commercial cultural village. The dancing is particularly good, and there is a small 'safari' park with snakes, crocodiles and other wild animals.

Durban's **Muti Market** (or traditional healers' market) is the Southern Hemisphere's biggest

OPPOSITE: *Zulu women use intricate beadwork to convey messages about their stages of life, such as being ready for marriage or being engaged or pregnant. Beadwork can also be used to create love letters or to signify mourning.*

ABOVE: *A visit to one of KZN's cultural villages, such as Shakaland, provides an opportunity to experience Zulu culture.*

THE PEOPLE

bazaar for traditional medicine. It is truly fascinating, if rather mind-boggling to Western sensibilities. While the piles of herbs and plants and rows of animal parts on the pavements – whole, chopped and dried – can be overwhelming, it is important to note that some 80% of South Africans happily make use of traditional medicine.

BELOW: *Traders and sangomas can be seen at the traditional Muti Market in Durban, where they consult with patients and sell herbal medicines.*

In the second week of September, young unmarried women from throughout the province arrive at eNyokeni Zulu Royal Palace for the **Annual Royal Reed Dance**, known as *woMhlanga* or *uMhlanga*. Here hundreds of bare-breasted maidens, adorned in time-honoured style and carrying long canes, dance in rows before the king and an assembled audience.

The ceremony celebrates the purity and fertility of the Zulu virgins who participate in it, and recognises the mutual respect between the royals and the Zulu nation. It also marks the contribution young women make to nation building, and historically was a time when the king chose a new bride. Taking photographs is strictly controlled.

Millions of black South Africans live in the townships surrounding the cities. A **township tour** allows an opportunity to meet the local people in their own homes and environments, and will usually take in the sites associated with the iNanda Heritage Trail – **Gandhi's settlement** at Phoenix, the **Ohlanga Institute** and **John Dube's Grave**.

A highlight of a township tour is visiting a hostel, which in apartheid times was where rural people were accommodated in urban areas when they came to work. They used to be single-sex dormitories but have been converted to accommodate families, and offer fascinating insight into the lives of many KNZ residents.

KwaDabeka Hostel in Clermont, said to be the largest in the Southern Hemisphere, houses some

15 000 people. Residents have set up informal retail outlets in the central part of the hostel, known with true Zulu humour as the CBD (Central Business District). Even with overcrowding and underlying poverty, the residents are always friendly and welcome visitors. Music blares, laundry hangs from windows and people sit around chatting with friends and neighbours. Tours usually end with a meal and cold beer at a local tavern.

Cool Runnings, a Caribbean-style reggae bar and restaurant, is an institution in Durban. This well-known and truly cosmopolitan pub is one of the few easily accessible places in the province where people of all races and backgrounds mix together in a relaxed and happy atmosphere. Play pool and jive with Zulu customers in the front bar, watch rowdy soccer and rugby games on television, or attend funky Thursday-night drum circles run by friendly Rastas.

The **Emnambithi Cultural Centre** has some great exhibits, including one devoted to the Ladysmith Black Mambazo choir that became world famous by singing with Paul Simon. Another display honours great local achievers such as world super-middleweight boxing champion Thulani 'Sugarboy' Malinga, artist Lallitha Jawahirilall and a Springbok shot-put athlete Veronica Abrahamse. There is also a small shop selling local arts and crafts.

INDIANS

After slavery was abolished in 1834, British settlers recruited indentured labour for their sugar, tea and coffee plantations. The first Indian labourers arrived in Natal in 1860, soon followed by Indian traders. After the indentured labourers were released from their three-year contracts, many elected to settle in the area and a thriving Indian community soon developed.

They brought with them their colourful culture and their food, dress, languages and religions.

ABOVE: *The annual Royal Reed Dance, in days gone by, was when the Zulu king would choose a new wife. These days, the revived ceremony promotes chastity and cultural morals.*

John Dube

John Dube founded the Natal Native Congress in 1900, which was later affiliated to the African National Congress (ANC). He also created the now famous Ohlanga High School and Institute, which offered black Africans quality education at a time when this was neglected. Dube's frequent criticism of the government resulted in his arrest during the Bhambatha Uprising of 1906. He died in 1946.

THE PEOPLE

BELOW: *The Sri Muruga Kovil in Phoenix, Durban, is dedicated to the Hindu deity Lord Muruga, who is popular with Tamil Hindus.*

BELOW RIGHT: *KZN Muslims are of Indian, Malaysian and Chinese descent, having come from Java as labourers.*

By 1865 there were about 5 300 Indians living in Durban alone. Today it is often said that KZN has the largest population of Indians living outside of India. While that may not strictly be true, it is possible that South Africa is home to the largest population of Indians in sub-Saharan Africa, and they continue to play an integral and important role in the cultural, political and economic life of the province.

Experiencing Indian culture

Many foreigners do not realise that Gandhi spent 21 years of his life in South Africa. Apart from his Phoenix settlement, there are a variety of sites and monuments to Gandhi throughout the province. Some of the smaller sites are the **Dundee Police Station**, where he was charged for his role in the 1913 protest march, and the **Hindu temple** in Dundee where he worshipped during the 1914 passive resistance campaign.

The **Durban Cultural and Documentation Centre** serves as a place of learning and research, preserving the history, culture and development of South Africans of Indian origin. It also promotes visual and performing arts. Original documents

THE PEOPLE

donated by Durban's Indian community are on display along with photographic exhibitions of the lives of indentured Indian labourers and Gandhi's stay in South Africa. Call in advance if you are planning to visit.

The Indian peoples are known for their colourful **festivals** and **ceremonies**, which provide a wonderful window into this vibrant culture (see Faiths of the People pp. 34 & 36).

EUROPEANS

White settlers began to arrive in the province in earnest in 1829, following British traders and missionaries who had come out to convert the natives. The warring Zulus initially tolerated the small settlement as it suited the ivory trade.

However, during the late 1830s, the Boers, disgruntled with the British in the Cape, trekked into the province and established the settlement of Pietermaritzburg.

They later claimed control of the small, strategic bay of Port Natal (now Durban), only to be ousted in 1843 when the British annexed the region. A series of territorial battles between British and Boer, Boer and Zulu, and British and Zulu resulted in the end of the Zulu empire in 1897 and British domination of the area.

Experiencing European culture

Many sugar barons became extremely wealthy, building fabulous colonial homes, many of which still exist today. The **Killie Campbell Museum**,

Mahatma Gandhi

Mohandas Gandhi, one of India's most famous sons, arrived in KZN in 1893 as a young, London-trained barrister. Refusing to leave the 'whites only' train carriage he was travelling in, he was evicted and spent the night in the cold waiting room of Pietermaritzburg Station, and declared in later life that 'my active non-violence began from that day'. He went on to establish a settlement and play a significant role in the early struggle years, and establish the passive resistance campaign. Loved the world over for his efforts, Mohandas is more commonly called by his honorific title of Mahatma Gandhi, *mahatma* meaning 'great soul' in Sanskrit.

Pietermaritzburg's statue of Mahatma Gandhi was erected to mark the centenary of the start of Gandhi's passive resistance campaign.

ABOVE: *The memorial at Isandlwana commemorates the Zulu warriors who fell while securing this important victory over the British.*

situated in a graceful Cape Dutch-inspired building in Durban, was built by Marshall Campbell.

Today, Campbell's home, Muckleneuk, located adjacent to the museum, houses rare and unique, internationally renowned archival resources known as the **Killie Campbell Africana Collections**. The collection includes the **Killie Campbell Africana Library** that preserves an excellent array of books, manuscripts and photographs depicting the history of the area, the **William Campbell Furniture and Picture Collection**, the **Mashu Museum of Ethnology** and the **Jo Thorpe Collection**.

Baynesfield Estate, which was founded in 1863 near Richmond, was the property of wealthy farmer Joseph Baynes until he bequeathed it to the public upon his death. Baynes made a great contribution to the development of agriculture in South Africa, most notably in pioneering the dairy industry and using dipping to save cattle from the deadly East Coast Fever, a disease carried by ticks.

Baynes' House and its beautiful gardens and maze can be visited by prior arrangement. His cattle dip (rumoured to have been built by the Mariannhill monks) and dairy can also be seen on site.

THE PEOPLE

The Battlefields

The largest concentration of battlefields in Southern Africa lies in the rolling grasslands and historic towns of northern KZN. Heroic and often tragic deeds took place here, significantly influencing the development of South Africa and its people. King Shaka's 12-year military reign in the early 19th century resulted in bloody battles as he sought control over various indigenous clans. Conflict later arose between the Voortrekkers and King Dingane, Shaka's successor. Similarly there were clashes between Brit and Boer, and Brit and Zulu.

The **Battle of Blood River/Ncome** (1838) is today commemorated by a poignant monument situated in the veld between Dundee and Vryheid and consists of 64 bronze ox-wagons arranged in the precise laager formation used during the battle. The Anglo–Zulu War (1879) saw another series of bloody battles, most famous of which were **Isandlwana** and **Rorke's Drift**.

The battle of **Spioenkop** (1900) is fascinating in that three unlikely men who went on to become great leaders were in attendance. General Louis Botha, later the first prime minister of the Union of South Africa, led the Boer forces. The later British prime minister Winston Churchill, in South Africa as a war correspondent at the time, served as a courier and Mahatma Gandhi was a stretcher bearer.

Still more wars took place in this region, including the First Anglo–Boer War (1880–81), the Second Anglo–Boer War (1899–1902), the Rebellion of Langalibalele (1873) and the Bhambatha Uprising (1906). There are several cemeteries, monuments and museums throughout the area, each with an intriguing historical tale to tell.

There are a number of well-located lodges from where the Battlefields can be explored. **Fugitives Drift Lodge** was home to the late raconteur David Rattray, whose lifelong passion for the Battlefields and the people of the province ensured the prominence of this region. **Isandlwana Lodge**, with its spectacular views of the sphinx-like Isandlwana Mountain, is another great place to stay, and the luxurious **SpionKop Lodge** offers tours around the Battlefields as well as great bird-watching, game viewing and sunset cruises on the Spioenkop Dam.

OPPOSITE: *Reenactments, such as this one of the Battle of Talana, are popular with tourists and all sectors of KZN society, and bring to life the province's rich history.*

BELOW: *A 1879 sketch by Melton Prior shows the British collecting their dead following their enormous defeat at the Battle of Isandlwana.*

3

FAITHS OF THE PEOPLE

Religion plays an important role in KZN, which is a melting pot of spiritual faiths. While almost 80% of residents practise a form of Christianity, there are also many followers of Islam, Hinduism, Judaism and African traditional beliefs, as well as a smattering of adherents of Buddhism.

FAITHS OF THE PEOPLE

PREVIOUS PAGE: *Prior Franz Pfanner, founder of the Mariannhill Monastery, is depicted in a statue on the site.*

BELOW: *Modern rural Zulu homesteads still tend to favour the traditional round design.*

OPPOSITE: *Members of Durban's Shembe community can often be seen worshipping outdoors on Saturday mornings.*

SHEMBE

Today, even though essentially Christian in nature, a number of African churches combine elements of their traditional beliefs with Christianity. The Shembe are one such group. Followers of Shembe believe that in 1910 Isaiah Shembe, prophet and founder of the Shembe Church, received a message from God on a mountain near iNanda, north of Durban. He named this sacred site Ekuphakameni, meaning the 'place of spiritual upliftment', and formed what became one of the first independent churches in Southern Africa. Today membership of the Shembe Church numbers approximately 400 000.

The Shembe citadel, Ebhohleni, overlooks iNanda Dam. However, Shembe places of worship throughout the province can generally be identified by an outdoor circle of white stones, often under trees, as the Shembe associate strongly with nature. Dance is considered a primary form of worship and is usually accompanied by slow drumbeats and the deep tones of an *imbomu*, a long horn many believe was the forerunner to the popular plastic vuvuzela used at football games.

Due to their close proximity to Mahatma Gandhi's home and printing works, the early Shembe adopted many of his ideas of self-sufficiency and pursued a strong, craft-based work ethic. They still adhere to these values today.

Three major **Shembe festivals**, as well as numerous other mass gatherings, are held annually and are well worth attending. The first, held on the first Sunday of every new year, is the 80-kilometre **pilgrimage** from the church headquarters at Ebhohleni up the 'Holy Mountain' of Nhlangakazi, a

Traditional African beliefs

Before missionaries brought the concept of the Christian god to Africa, the Zulus looked to *uMvelinqangi* ('he who came first') as the all-powerful creator. *uMvelinqangi* could not be approached directly but rather through the medium of the ancestors, who in turn could only be accessed through a traditional diviner or sangoma.

These ancestral spirits, known as *amadlozi* or *amathongo* – or the *izithunzi* ('shadows' or 'shades' of the underworld) – are still central to traditional African beliefs.

FAITHS OF THE PEOPLE

ritual that celebrated its centenary in 2010. Pilgrims walk for three days, and upon arrival at the plateau colourful services with much energetic singing take place.

There are also two **month-long festivals**. In July, visitors to Ekuphakameni, and some other areas in the province, are welcome to observe the spectacular festivities of shield-waving warriors, men in kilts and pith helmets, bare-breasted maidens and traditional matrons all in matching finery, as well as beautifully choreographed dancing. A similar ceremony takes place in October in Judea, eShowe, when some 25 000 Shembe followers come together with their traditional leader. Both events culminate on the last weekend of their respective months with a prayer service on the Saturday and a spectacular, not-to-be-missed, mass traditional dance on the Sunday.

Visitors who are unable to attend any of the festivals can liaise with a tour operator (through KZN Tourism) to go along to any regular Shembe day of worship. The Shembe are used to visitors and always make them feel welcome, but please respect their ways and remove your shoes before entering the church circle.

MUSLIMS

The first Muslims to arrive in then Natal were Malaysian and Chinese labourers who were brought from Java to work on the sugar estates by the Umzinto Sugar Company in 1858. Soon after, Indian indentured labourers began to land in Durban, a minority of whom were also Muslim.

From these original few, a large and influential Muslim population has grown, having an enormous impact on the life of the province. By 1904, there were 40 Indian schools in Durban alone, 10 of which were privately administered by

> ### Interesting ceremonies
> Other traditional ceremonies can be discretely witnessed on Durban's beachfront, as many baptisms or cleansing ceremonies take place at sunrise. These are private rituals, so visitors are kindly asked to keep their distance and not disturb the participants. During Easter and Christmas, various religious groups including Shembe and Zionists come from all over the country to worship at the water's edge, arriving in their colourful church uniforms to sing and drum as the sun rises over the sea. It is a wonderful sight to behold.
>
> **Khekhekhe Mthethwa**, one of Zululand's most famous traditional healers, was renowned for his ability to work with snakes. People came from near and far for healing. Although Khekhekhe has since passed away, the annual **Snake Ceremony** he established is still observed in February each year at Ngudwini near eShowe, and is attended by hundreds of people. This is a fantastic ritual, giving true insight into authentic Zulu culture. Visitors are always welcomed, and may organise attendance through Zululand Eco-Adventures.

OPPOSITE: *The beautiful Hazrath Soofie Saheb Masjid in Riverside, Durban North, is a heritage site, and while Muslims in general worship in it, it is also the headquarters of the International Sufi Order.*

28

FAITHS OF THE PEOPLE

the Muslim community. The RK Khan Hospital and the ML Sultan Technical College, precursor to the Durban University of Technology, are examples of other great institutions that were established by the Muslim community.

Another feat of the community was the construction of the **Jummah Mosque** on Durban's Dr Yusuf Dadoo Street (former Grey Street). From humble beginnings in 1884, the mosque has been enlarged and extended over the years to allow for the steady increase in Muslim worshippers, and at one stage it was the largest in the Southern Hemisphere.

With its fascinating mix of Islamic and colonial style, the Jummah Mosque is now a landmark feature of Durban's city centre. Non-followers of Islam are welcome to enter the sacred site and admire the gilt-domed minarets and marbled worship hall. This is best done outside of prayer time, and visitors should dress accordingly – shoulders should be covered and female visitors should preferably wear a long skirt or dress to cover their legs. A tour includes some history of the Muslim community, architecture of the mosque and an introduction to Islamic beliefs (see Creative Thinking p. 41).

JEWS

Approximately 0,1% of Durban's population follow Judaism, which accounts for some 10 500 people.

BELOW: *The massive Jummah Mosque is an important place of worship for Durban's Muslim community.*

BELOW RIGHT: *Many of KZN's mosques are heritage sites, such as the Jummah Mosque in Durban.*

FAITHS OF THE PEOPLE

The **Durban Jewish Club** is a lovely old red-tiled building, built in 1913 as a general meeting place for the Jewish community in the growing town. During World War II, more than two million servicemen passed through its doors, as it was used as a canteen for the Allied forces. It is still the centre of much activity, not just for the Jewish community but for Durbanites in general, with classical music concerts, photographic exhibitions and many other cultural events regularly on offer.

A **Garden of Remembrance** and **Holocaust Centre** have been established on the premises in memory of the almost six million Jews who lost their lives due to Nazi persecution. The centre is particularly poignant in South Africa because of the inevitable comparisons that can be drawn between the oppression endured by Jews internationally and the human rights violations suffered locally by black, coloured and Indian people as a result of apartheid, both born of the attitude that some ethnicities or races are superior to others. Volunteers have been trained to take school groups and other visitors through the centre.

CHRISTIANS

Following the annexation of Natal as a British colony in 1843, Christian missionary groups started to trickle into the area. Among others, these included

BELOW LEFT: *The Star of David, seen here on a menorah, is an ancient symbol of the Jewish faith.*

BELOW: *The Holocaust Centre is one of Durban's most poignant and beautiful museums, highlighting issues of prejudice and racism.*

FAITHS OF THE PEOPLE

British Protestants, Norwegian and Swedish Lutherans, as well as Roman Catholics.

Perhaps the most notable of these missions is that of the **Mariannhill Monastery** that was established by Trappist monks in 1885, which went on to become the largest Trappist settlement in the world. Located just outside Durban, in Mariannhill, the monastery grounds offer shelter from the hustle and bustle of modern living, transporting visitors to a simpler, more peaceful era. Tours can be arranged or visitors can wander around on their own before having tea in the tranquil tea garden.

The Trappist monks were very proactive in spreading their faith. By 1909 there were 49 Catholic mission stations throughout the area, most of which had been founded by the 'Mariannhillers'. Although many of these once-beautiful structures are now somewhat run down, they are still well worth a visit. Predominantly with striking red-brick architecture, they are usually located in stunning locations with serene surroundings. It is possible to stay overnight at many of the mission stations, provided bookings are made in advance.

Richenau Mission, on the Pholela River en route to Underberg, was established in 1886 by Mariannhill monks. The interior of the lovely church is painted in the Germanic style and there is rudimentary overnight accommodation. The very rural **Centekow Mission**, established in 1888 near Creighton, has the most incredible buildings – visitors would not be amiss to feel they have somehow been teleported back in time to medieval Europe. The mission is extremely active in the rural community, engaging in much charitable work. If possible, attend a Palm Sunday celebration around March or April, and watch as a priest arrives on donkey.

Other mission churches worth a mention are the **Lourdes Mission**, which was one of the biggest of its kind a hundred years ago, and **Mariathal Mission**, about 8 kilometres from iXopo. Mariathal has been lovingly restored and converted into the King's Grant Country Retreat guesthouse, which has conference and wedding facilities. **Maria Ratschitz Mission**, outside Dundee, has also been skillfully restored, with all its frescos repainted by German artisans. Interestingly, it was not established by Mariannhill monks.

To attend any of the major ceremonies on the Christian calendar, such as Easter or Christmas, at one of these rural mission stations is an experience of a lifetime. General services can be enjoyed on any Sunday throughout the province, and visitors are always welcome, even in small rural villages. If possible, join a service with a predominantly Zulu congregation, as the singing is sure to provoke goose bumps. There are also many beautiful and historic churches throughout rural KZN, each with its own story relating to a major, or sometimes just

interesting, historical incident. An example is the **Church of the Vow** in Pietermaritzburg, which has been converted into a museum. Before the Battle of Blood River/Ncome, Boer leader Andries Pretorius vowed that should they defeat the Zulus, he would have a church built in commemoration. Today the church is part of the Voortrekker Museum.

HINDUS

Devotees to the Hindu faith arrived on the same boat as Muslims in 1858 and soon made their mark on the province, building temples and establishing communities as their indentured labour contracts came to an end. Brightly painted towers of Hindu temples pop out behind buildings and trees nearly everywhere in the province. Visitors seeking insight into the Hindu culture and religion should explore these beautiful buildings, easily done in Durban, either independently or on a tour. The three highlighted below are all heritage sites.

The **Sri Ambalavanaar Alayam Temple** on Bellair Road, Cato Manor, is one of the oldest shrines in the area, with Hindu gods Vishnu, Shiva and Ganesha brightly adorning the walls. The original structure was erected in 1875, making it the first Hindu temple to be built in Africa, however, being on the banks of the Umbilo River, it was damaged beyond repair by the 1905 floods.

The present structure, whose beautiful cellar doors were salvaged from the original, was built in 1947. If possible, attend the annual fire-walking ceremony, held around April.

OPPOSITE: *A gentle depiction of Mary provides comfort to followers of Catholicism.*

ABOVE: *The cloisters at Mariannhill Monastery provide quiet, contemplative spaces away from the commotion of city life.*

FAITHS OF THE PEOPLE

RIGHT: *Colourful deities and elaborate architectural features adorn KZN's many Hindu temples, such as the Sri Muruga Kovil in Phoenix, Durban.*

OPPOSITE: *The impressive ceiling of the Sri Sri Radhanath Temple of Understanding in Chatsworth depicts scenes of Lord Krishna's life.*

Another beautiful temple is the **Sri Ganesha Temple** at Mount Edgecombe, built in 1899 by Kistappa Reddy who came to the country as an indentured labourer. The deep mouldings and sculptures at the entrance gate take on a three-dimensional quality in the right light.

The **Sri Jagannath Puri Temple** near Tongaat (not to be confused with the New Sri Jagannath Puri Temple, a Hare Krishna temple in Phoenix) was modelled on the famous temple of the same name on the banks of the Ganges River in India. It was built by a Hindu priest and Sanskrit scholar, Shiskishan Maharaj, who worked as an indentured labourer. Particularly interesting is the image at the entrance of Jagannath (the war-like god to whom the temple is dedicated), which slowly becomes apparent as the temple is approached, showing the deity in all his fearsome glory.

Even if you are not a follower of the faith, Hindu festivals are all-inclusive, colourful and fascinating. The **Porridge Festival**, a 10-day celebration in July or August, is so called because gifts of oatmeal with milk, coconuts and pumpkins are offered to the Mariamman, the goddess of disease and rain. There are at least 16 temples in KZN dedicated to this deity. Although very few temples follow the rituals of goat

FAITHS OF THE PEOPLE

and chicken sacrifice, there are a few, such as the **Sri Mariamman Temple** at Isipingo Rail, which do.

Diwali, the **Festival of Lights**, is a five-day celebration of the triumph of good over evil, in memory of Lord Rama's defeat of the demon king Ravana. Although it is predominantly a home-based ritual, there are a number of fun, public events, mostly involving fabulous fireworks displays. This festival takes place in October or November, and devotees light symbolic lamps and candles throughout the period.

The night preceding the main event of **Holi**, the **Festival of Colours**, celebrating the arrival of spring, entails lighting massive bonfires that symbolise the destruction of the evil demon Holika. This is followed by light-hearted flinging of coloured powders and water at friends. Being a Southern Hemisphere city the festival takes place at the end of summer in Durban, around March.

Hinduism dates back some 5 000 years, with Ayurveda, the ancient medicinal treaties of the Hindus, being the oldest, continually practised medicinal system in the world. To experience some of the delights of this methodology, the **SanAquam Urban Ayurvedic Spa** in Durban offers *Snehana*, a full-body massage using specific massage sequences and a specially prepared blend of herbal oils; *Bashpaswedana*, a traditional steam bath; and *Shirodhara*, where precisely prepared herbal oil is rhythmically poured in a steady warm steam onto the forehead, or the third eye, as well as other Ayurvedic treatments.

OPPOSITE LEFT: *People from all over the world come to enjoy peace and meditation at the Buddhist Retreat Centre outside iXopo in KZN's beautiful Midlands.*

OPPOSITE RIGHT: *Peaceful statues of Siddhārtha Gautama, the Buddha or Enlightened One, can be found in the gentle gardens of the Buddhist Retreat Centre.*

Hare Krishnas

Krishna consciousness has its roots in the Vedic scriptures of India, and as such is in many ways similar to Hinduism, although there are some important differences. The movement was brought to Durban in 1975 with the arrival of its spiritual leader and founder, AC Bhaktivedanta Swami Prabhupada, and since then it has grown substantially in popularity.

The **Sri Sri Radhanath Temple of Understanding** in Chatsworth has large steeples, unique in this country, designed by the International Society of Krishna Consciousness. Inside, the domed roof is adorned with massive depictions of the life of Lord Krishna. Downstairs is a wonderful restaurant, renowned for its delicious vegetarian food and reasonable prices.

There are many festivals and celebrations on the Hare Krishna calendar throughout the year, the largest being the annual four-day **Ratha Yatra Festival**, also known as the **Festival of Chariots**, which is in March or April each year and coincides with the Christian Easter. The focal point of the procession, which honours several deities, is generally an enormous red chariot pulled through the city by devotees, and a huge gathering takes place on Durban's beachfront honouring Lord Krishna. The festival consists of fabulous food, dancing and music. Stalls selling Indian cultural items and delicacies line the beachfront during the weekend.

A second, and equally important, festival is the **Janmastami Festival**, which celebrates the birth of Lord Krishna. It is held in September or October each year.

BUDDHISTS

Worldwide interest in Buddhism began when the Dalai Lama, leader of the world's Buddhists, went into self-exile in 1959 following the Chinese invasion of Tibet. The **Buddhist Retreat Centre** in iXopo, founded in 1980, is arguably the most famous Buddhist institution in South Africa, being awarded heritage status by former president Nelson Mandela. It is enormously popular with people of all faiths from all walks of life. Courses covering basic Buddhism, pottery and kite-making are run during weekends while longer retreats also take place. The centre is also celebrated for its wholesome vegetarian meals.

The nearby **Woza Moya Project**, which provides services in the areas of home-based care, orphan intervention and food security for those affected by HIV/Aids, was initiated by former staff of the centre. It is fascinating to visit, as it provides a truly insightful perspective on the lives of people living in this poverty-stricken, rural region of the province.

4

CREATIVE THINKING

KZN has a vibrant array of the arts. The diversity of its residents has resulted in an eclectic range of styles in architecture, painting, drawing, sculpture, pottery, crafts, theatre, music and dance, and art lovers are unlikely to run out of creative entertainment or inventive delights.

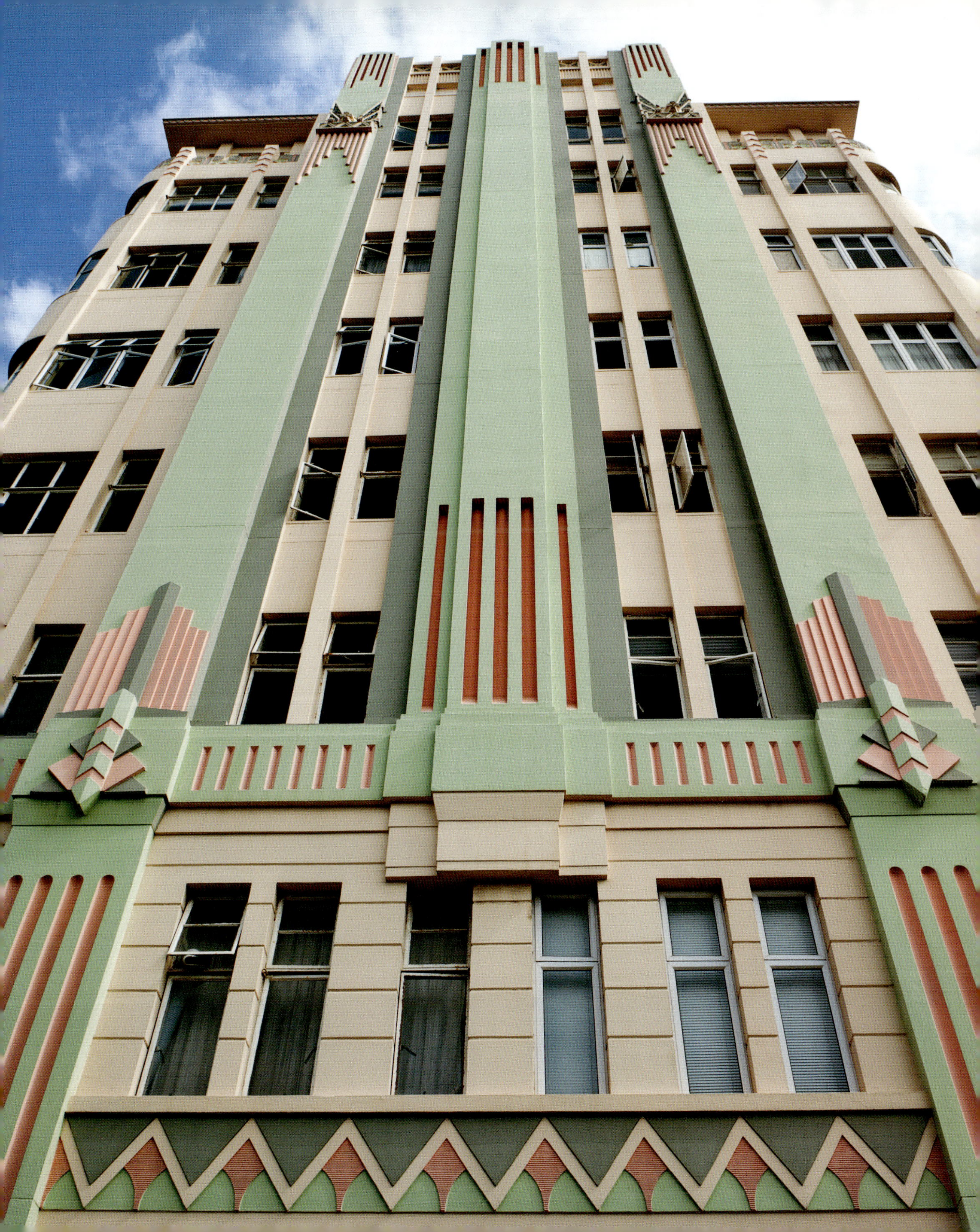

CREATIVE THINKING

PREVIOUS PAGE: *Durban has approximately 106 Art Deco buildings, including Surrey Mansions, designed in 1937 by architect William B Barboure.*

BELOW: *Traditional Zulu homesteads, or izindlu, are round with thatched roofs.*

BELOW RIGHT: *Rural people have innovative and creative building methods for constructing their homes, using natural materials from their immediate surroundings.*

ARCHITECTURE

Not only is there great cultural, religious and racial diversity across the province, but there has been an array of international influences on the area in the last two centuries. One of the physical facets of KZN that wonderfully mirrors these effects is its buildings, as evident in the choice of architectural styles for homes, industry-related structures and places of worship. There are many landmark showpieces, from commercial to residential, and contemporary to historic.

Historic

The oldest recorded residential structures in the area would be ***izindlu***, the traditional Zulu grass 'beehive' houses. While these are no longer popularly used, reconstructions can be seen at cultural villages and some of the Zululand museums, such as the **Ondini Historical Complex** near uLundi.

When the Voortrekkers settled in their Republic of Natalia (now Pietermaritzburg) in 1839 they finally moved out of the ox-wagons that had been their homes for the previous four years and constructed **wattle-and-daub houses**. These structures were made up of a woven lattice of wooden strips that were stuck together with a combination of wet soil, clay, sand, dung and straw. While there are no complete structures of this kind remaining intact, an example of a hardier **shale house**, built circa 1840, can be found at the **Voortrekker/Msunduzi Museum** in Langalibalele Street. The structure, which has a thatched roof and a front facade of several 12-paned casement windows, is the oldest double-storey house in Pietermaritzburg.

Also famous in KZN are the **red-brick colonial buildings**, many of which are concentrated in Pietermaritzburg where various buildings were constructed to meet the growing town's needs.

Good ones to see are City Hall, the railway station, Tatham Art Gallery (which used to be the Supreme Court) and the Alexander Road Police Station. Tours are available and well worth the time.

While in Pietermaritzburg, stop by the **Diamond Jubilee Pavilion**, which was built to celebrate Queen Victoria's 60th year on the throne. It faces the picturesque City Oval cricket stadium in Alexander Park.

Religious

Domed Islamic mosques and pointed Hindu temples punctuate the skyline almost everywhere across the province. Particularly delightful is the exquisite **Sufi Mosque**, on the banks of the Klip River in Ladysmith, which has been proclaimed a heritage site. Jamaloodeen, the mosque's master builder, is said to have designed the building in his head, sketching plans for the day's work in the sand each morning.

In 1916, another famed master builder, Alaga Pillay, was brought from India to build the **Vishnu Temple** in Durban. He was also commissioned to build the **Hindu Thirukootam and Sri Ganaser Temple** in Ladysmith. It is a fine example of colonial, verandah-style buildings with the classic Indian lotus-form dome.

There are also many interesting Christian mission churches in the province worth seeing (see Faiths of the People p. 32).

ABOVE: *Pietermaritzburg's famous red-brick City Hall is an outstanding example of colonial architecture.*

CREATIVE THINKING

Contemporary

Of a somewhat more modern nature are Durban's renowned **Art Deco buildings**. Take a tour with the **Durban Art Deco Society** to enjoy the many noteworthy structures embodying the non-conformist, anti-establishment movement that spread throughout the world from 1925–40.

Great examples are Surrey Mansions and Cheviot Court on the Berea, Essop Moosa Building and Arbee Mansions in the old Grey Street area of town, now called Dr Yusuf Dadoo Street, and the Broadwindsor, Enterprise Building and Hollywood Court in central Durban.

On the link road between the N3 and the Hluhluwe-iMfolozi Game Reserve, look out for East Coast Architects' **Africa Centre for Health and Population Studies**, which received awards from both the South African Institute of Architects and the KZN Institute for Architecture.

Situated in this rural setting to be close to the people being studied to allow for better insight into their hardships and health issues, the building consists of four pods surrounding a central atrium. According to those who work there, all those who visit the centre visibly have their spirits lifted by the well-thought-out building that harmoniously integrates technology and nature.

VISUAL ARTS
Fine art

KZN has some of South Africa's most impressive art galleries, which boast an enviable collection of fine art. The **Tatham Art Gallery** in Pietermaritzburg, housed in the old 1875 Supreme Court Building and adjacent 1852 Presbyterian church, has a superb collection of 18th- and 19th-century South African, British and French art.

Pietermaritzburg also hosts the annual **Art in the Park**, a popular outdoor art exhibition in which 60-or-so top South African artists showcase their work, usually in May or June. A variety of painting mediums are represented, as well as photography and glassworks.

Durban Art Gallery, in Durban City Hall, has a permanent collection specialising in international and contemporary South African art. Not only does the gallery host a wide range of shows of national and international interest, but it is famous for its funky Red Eye @rt fundraising events, held a few times a year. Aimed at a younger audience, attendees can eat, listen to live music, watch a little street theatre and generally have a good time.

There are several outstanding private galleries in Durban, such as **The African Art Centre** on Florida Road, a non-profit organisation with a well-established reputation for its quality art and support of rural up-and-coming artists. **The BAT Centre**, a non-profit organisation in the Small Craft Harbour, provides working studios for artists. It also has gallery space and a shop that sells their high-quality crafts.

artSPACE and **KZNSA** (KwaZulu-Natal Society of Arts) galleries, in Stamford Hill and Glenwood respectively, have regular new exhibits. The latter also has a popular gallery shop and restaurant-cum-coffee shop outside under the trees.

The **Durban University of Technology Gallery** rotates exhibitions regularly, showcasing the work of established artists as well as that of art and design students and community projects.

Arts and crafts

The arts-and-crafts sector plays an important economic role in the province, providing much-needed employment to many locals. Indeed, about 200 000 people are afforded a source of income through this industry, with some 40 000 crafters being involved in craft activities at various levels of commercial intensity.

In particular, the sector generates opportunities for rural women – some of the most economically disadvantaged people in KZN – who are often isolated from traditional work prospects.

The market for traditional crafts is on its way to being successfully developed, but there is still some way to go. The Zulu people bring generations'

OPPOSITE: *The famous waterproof baskets made by the women of Hlabisa in rural Zululand have become collectors' items.*

ABOVE LEFT: *The Tatham Art Gallery, once KZN's Supreme Court, houses some of the province's most fascinating art collections.*

ABOVE: *Durban's BAT Centre offers facilities to both rural and urban artists and crafters.*

The Midlands Meander

The Midlands Meander was the first craft route to be established in the country and is arguably still the most famous. Informally founded in the 1970s by an enterprising group of crafters living in the gently rolling countryside between Pietermaritzburg and the Drakensberg Mountains, the association became more structured in 1985. In their desire to live an authentic, simple lifestyle and break away from the rat race of the established art world, they decided to try encourage visitors to come to their studios. Increasingly, so-called 'corporate refugees' are setting up businesses in the area, drawn by the tranquillity of the lifestyle.

While there are several possible routes to take, the Midlands Meander roughly covers the area between Hilton or Howick in the southeast and Mooi River in the northwest, and includes some 200 venues. It is no longer confined to just arts and crafts outlets, but also includes herb farms, country inns, B&Bs, guesthouses, restaurants and even a number of health spas. Excellent maps are available from Meander outlets or the Midlands Meander office.

Apart from the many opportunities to purchase and appreciate arts and crafts, there is a multitude of fantastic events in the area throughout the year. When planning a trip, refer to the informative and up-to-date Midland Meander website (see contact list) to see what coincides. A wonderful option is the **Hilton Arts Festival**, around about September each year, which brings the best of South African theatre to KZN.

Hilton is also where **The Rotunda Farm Stall** is located, a great place to relax with a cappuccino. Afterwards, browse the lovely wooden furniture by **Johnson Bros Country Furniture** nearby. Another fine craft outlet is the **Glass Cuttings Shop and Gallery**, which offers a selection of high-quality, hand-made glass products.

In Merrivale, **Hi-Fly Kites**, specialising in children's kites, trick kites and power kites, is the ultimate stop for kite enthusiasts. Nearby in Howick, **The Weaver's Hut** is an outlet for tightly woven woollen rugs made by Zulu women on frame looms, using the age-old tradition of hand weaving.

Groundcover Leather Company is situated in a lovely old wood-and-iron house in Curry's Post, near Lions River. They make comfortable, funky shoes and other leather items. In the front of the shop is a whimsical pixie sculpture by well-known KZN artist, Abbo Hall. On the western side of the N3, in Lions River, are **Lona's Pianos**, dealing in beautifully restored upright and grand pianos, and **Spiral Blue**, which sells wonderfully colourful and exotic items, great for gifts. Nearby in Dargle, **The Lavender Co.** sells luxurious body products and essential oils, which are grown and distilled on the farm.

Shuttleworth Weavers in Fort Nottingham now export their quality carpets, curtains, clothing and throws hand spun in wool, cotton and some modern fibres. **Born in Africa** in Balgowan manufactures hand-stitched leather shoes, outdoor and children's clothing and African crafts, and also has a delicious deli. **The Candle Dipping Shop** in Nottingham Road is a great option for children.

Visitors can buy crafts along the Midlands Meander or acquire creative skills of their own. They can also watch artists at work at places such as at the Ardmore Ceramic Art studio in Caversham, which has gained international acclaim though its fascinating combination of traditional Zulu art styles with modern techniques.

CREATIVE THINKING

worth of skills to the industry, and while many crafters continue making and selling traditional crafts informally on roadsides, others have received more formal training.

The Wetland Crafts initiative, part of the Wetlands Authority's Social Economic and Environmental Development (SEED) unit, provides guidance for crafters in the iSimangaliso Wetland Park area on product development and quality. The initiative also assists them with selling their products to commercial operators.

Although many vendors now also sell a variety of cheap imported knick-knacks, there is still some good, authentic beadwork and basketware to be found. The **Umnini Craft Village**, on the N2 South just past aManzimtoti, has stalls selling massive grass mats, pots, beadwork, wooden items and many other traditional arts and crafts.

All along the N2 North, towards Maputaland, there are various excellent craft markets. There are also often markets situated at the entrances to reserves, such as iSimangaliso Wetland and Hluhluwe-iMfolozi parks. Look out for roadside vendors selling wooden meat platters, dolphin mobiles as well as traditional *fonya* baskets, which are used to catch fish.

Zulu pottery

Among the Zulu, pot making has traditionally been the work of women, many of whom are master potters. These experts know exactly where to find the best clay, what firing methods produce different colours and how to etch designs.

There are various kinds of pots that are created, each serving specific functions. *Imbiza*, the enormous pots used for brewing beer, are usually set into the ground and never moved. When the beer is to be consumed, usually passed around among a circle of men to share, it is either served in the bigger *ukhamba* or the smaller *umancishana*, known as the 'stingy' pot. If a visitor is served beer from an *umancishana*, it is a cue that he is not expected to stay long! Both of these beer pots are commonly patterned on the side, not only for aesthetic reasons but more practically to give them grip, preventing them from slipping from one's hands.

Water pots are easily recognisable by their neck or curved mouth, which are designed to prevent splashing.

Many rural Zulu people are skilled potters, famous for their functional and decorative clay pots, such as this ukhamba *pot used for drinking beer.*

ABOVE: *A variety of productions, such as* My Fair Lady, *are shown throughout the year in KZN.*

The Valley of a Thousand Hills has many excellent tourism development and job-creation projects. Try **Amandla Beadwork**, **1000 Hills Craft Village** (where Israel's Wire Art is) and **Hillcrest Aids Centre & Craft Shop**.

Another good craft region is around Port Edward. Apart from exploring the various craft shops, Palm Beach's **Bauchop Custom Knives and Swords** shop, of internationally acclaimed knife and sword maker Robert Bauchop, is definitely worth a visit.

PERFORMING ARTS
Theatre

KZN's cultural life is enhanced by its many wonderful theatres, such as the **Playhouse Theatre Complex**. Located in Durban's Anton Lembede Street (former Smith Street), the Playhouse showcases grand theatrical events.

The **Elizabeth Sneddon Theatre** is attached to the University of KZN in Durban, and although smaller than the Playhouse it is no less important, hosting Durban's annual Time of the Writer (March), Poetry Africa (September/October) and Durban International Film Festival (July/August) events.

Another theatre worth visiting, also located at the university, is the excellent **Hexagon Theatre**.

Supper theatre is very popular in the province. **Catalina Theatre** on Wilson's Wharf in Durban is small and intimate with decks overlooking the harbour. **The Barnyard Theatres** are concept dinner theatres replicated throughout the country, Durban's local being in Gateway. Other Durban options include the **Dockyard Supper Theatre** on Musgrave Road and **The Rhumbelow Theatre** in Umbilo, which hosts revues, drag shows and musicals. Smaller, more rural towns throughout KZN use their town or school halls for theatre productions.

Music

Venues throughout the province host live music, often featuring outstanding local musicians, many of whom have achieved not just national but international recognition. Ladysmith Black Mambazo, the group made famous for singing internationally with Paul Simon, specialises in an *iSicathamiya* style, without instrumental backing and including Zulu dance moves.

ABOVE: *The beautiful, Tudor-style Playhouse Theatre is one of Durban's premier venues.*

Busi Mhlongo also gained international acclaim, along with enormous local affection, for her spectacular voice. The likes of Nibs van der Spuy and Guy Buttery, *maskanda* giant Phuzekhemisi, jazz pianist Melvin Peters and the legendary Madala Kunene all play in their home province.

A great location to see musicians in action is the **Rainbow Restaurant** in Pinetown, which during apartheid was one of the only venues showcasing black musicians. Jazz venues include the **Zulu Jazz Lounge** at the Playhouse Theatre Complex, **The Centre for Jazz and Popular Music** at the University of KZN, **Yossi's Café** in Glenwood and **Eden on Essenwood**, Durban, which hosts musicians every Friday, Saturday and Sunday.

Durban's **Cafe Vacca Matta** at the Suncoast Casino & Entertainment World is a trendy dance club that has several event nights throughout the week, including live rock bands on Tuesdays. Another popular venue for live rock is the **Thunder**

Boswells Building

Something of interest relating to theatre is the Boswells Building in Dundee, built as the Biggarsberg Unity Lodge in 1898. This heritage site is the last remaining pre-1900 theatre in the province and is unique both historically and architecturally.

ABOVE: *The internationally renowned Drakensberg Boys' Choir demonstrates gumboot dancing during one of their regular performances in Champagne Valley.*

Road Rock Diner on Durban's Florida Road where some of South Africa's finest musicians perform.

Music lovers should be sure not to miss out on a performance by the world renowned **Drakensberg Boys' Choir** – often mentioned in the same breath as the Vienna and Harlem boys' choirs. During term time, when the boys are not on tour, there are regular performances at the state-of-the-art school theatre in Champagne Valley, which members of the public can attend. The **Music in the Mountains Festival** takes place during April or May and the magnificent **Christmas concerts** precede the festive season.

Afro-gospel music is huge in South Africa and performances are extremely moving. Ask around about local churches that have gospel singing in their Sunday service and go along.

The annual **Splashy Fen** festival has thousands of people gathering to enjoy contemporary music – mostly folk and rock – in the Southern Drakensberg. Held over the Easter long weekend in March or April, most people make a short holiday of it, camping with their friends on the riverbanks or hillsides surrounding the marquee, open-air stages and craft market.

Dance

Look out for any performances by the Fantastic Flying Fish Dance Company, The Flatfoot Dance Company, Siwela Sonke Dance Theatre, Phenduka Dance Theatre and the Nateshwar Dance Academy, which has branches around the province teaching the ancient art of Indian dance.

Beatrice Street YMCA in downtown Durban is one of the best places to see *iSicathamiya* – a dance form with its roots in rural Zulu culture. Competitive performances begin any time after 22:00 on a Saturday night and usually continue until about 07:00 the next morning. A large variety of groups perform, each entertaining with two or three original songs. Go with a guide who can explain the fascinating history of the dance form and explain the rules of the competition. There is also an annual National *iSicathamiya* Competition at the Playhouse Theatre Complex in about September.

Many of the original dances told battle stories, but these days they tend to reflect more modern cultural issues.

The *indlamu* is a traditional war dance most commonly associated with Zulu culture, performed to drums by men in full traditional attire. The *ingoma* is performed by boys and girls and is often danced in transition ceremonies denoting life stages.

Gumboot dancing is also popular. Interestingly, it developed on Durban's docks before being transferred to the mines. Old and new types of dance are sometimes fused.

BELOW: *Dance, music and theatre in KZN are influenced by the rich diversity of its people. Seen here is a performance of the* Lion of the East *at the Playhouse Theatre.*

5

PLAYING GAMES

Sport is an integral part of life in KZN, and Durban in particular actively markets itself as the sporting capital of the country. The great climate lends itself to this, as do the international-standard sporting facilities and the numerous world-class events that take place throughout the province.

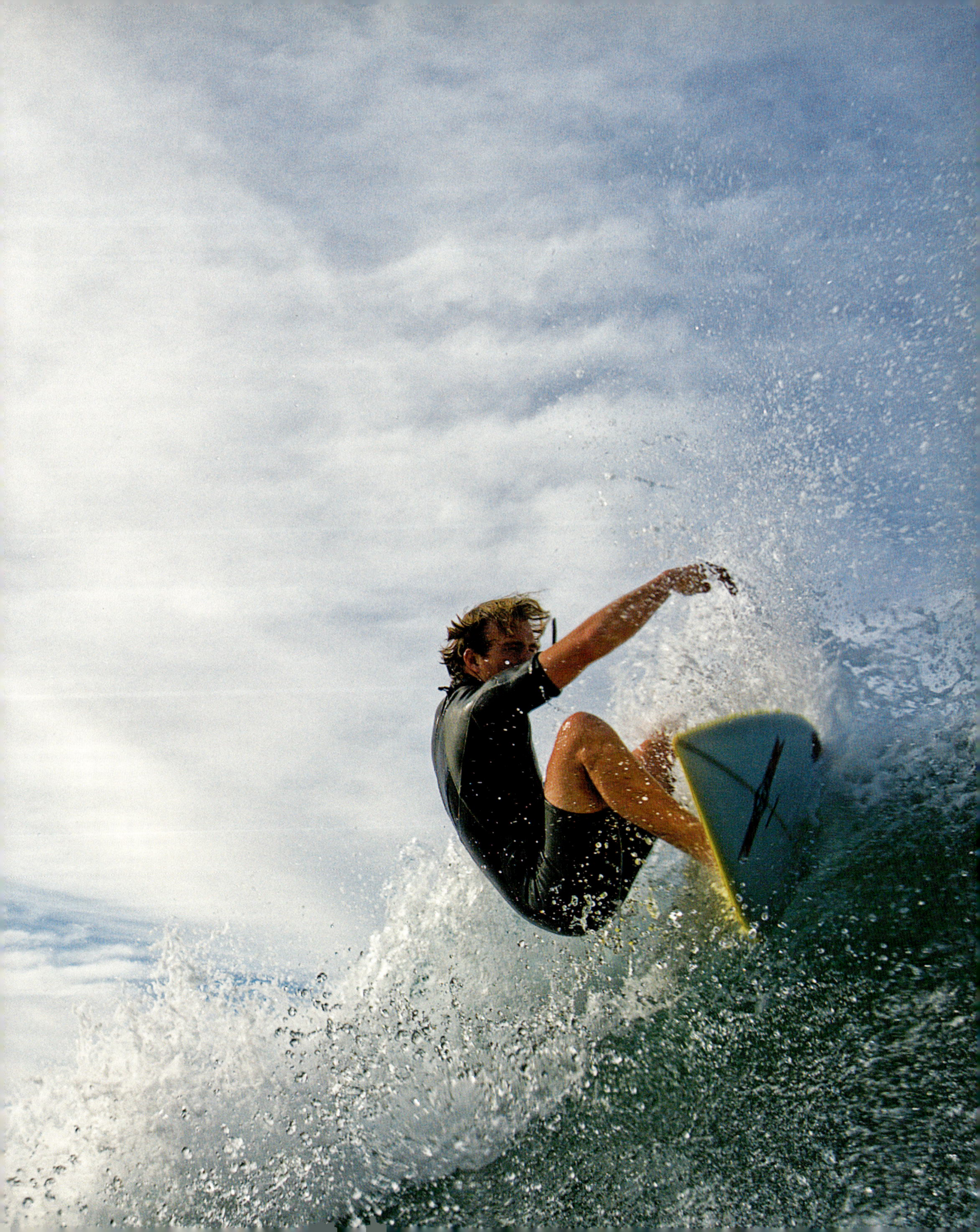

PLAYING GAMES

PREVIOUS PAGE: *KZN is something of a surfer's paradise, with warm water and a variety of beach and reef breaks suitable for all levels of expertise.*

BELOW: *Participants in the Dusi Canoe Marathon paddle down Camp's Drift Weir, one of the many exciting obstacles along the Msunduzi River.*

RACES AND EVENTS

The three-day **Dusi Canoe Marathon** is held on the Msunduzi River in January each year during the rainy season when water levels are high. Because the race has become so popular since its inception in the early 1960s, organisers have had to restrict numbers.

The paddlers set off from Pietermaritzburg in batches, negotiating rapids and weirs all the way to Blue Lagoon in Durban. They must sometimes run, carrying their canoes over rough terrain and hills until there is a safe place to return to the water. Thousands of supporters cheer from the riverbanks and join the paddlers at the stop-off points every evening.

Race organisers have made good use of the high-profile event to educate the public about water pollution and wise water-use practices.

The annual **Comrades Marathon**, a running event that commemorates fallen comrades of World War I, is usually held sometime between May and July, in the cooler months. Like the Dusi Canoe Marathon, it is held between the two cities of Durban and Pietermaritzburg, although the race direction is alternated annually. More than 20 000 runners from all over the country – and indeed from all over the world – participate in this gruelling, approximately 88-kilometre race.

PLAYING GAMES

While not everyone has the stamina to take on an ultra marathon of this nature, there is no need to miss out on the action. Join the throng of spectators who are up at sunrise, setting up their deck chairs and picnics on the side of the road to cheer the weary athletes on.

The 106-kilometre **Amashovashova** is one of the premier road cycle races in KZN, following much the same route as the Comrades Marathon. Alternatives affiliated with the main event include a 38-kilometre Family Fun Ride, two mountain bike events of 70 and 35 kilometres each, and some shorter rides for children.

A superb event is the **Karkloof Classic Mountain Bike Festival** in the Midlands in May. Apart from the main 75-kilometre **Karkloof Classic Marathon**, the festival offers a series of events, including a night ride, cross country race, family fun ride and cycle sprint shoot out, which encompasses a 400-metre obstacle course with jumps.

Two other great mountain bike events are the 75-kilometre **Giant's Castle MTB Challenge**, in the uKhahlamba-Drakensberg Park in April, and the 55-kilometre **iMfolozi Big 5 MTB Challenge**, in the Hluhluwe-iMfolozi Park in July or August, both made exciting by the proximity of wild game.

BELOW: *The diverse terrain throughout the province offers mountain bikers endless possibilities for adventure.*

PLAYING GAMES

RIGHT: *The Moses Mabhida Stadium, with its fabulous SkyCar, is an outstanding sports arena.*

The **Midmar Mile** swim race at Midmar Dam near Howick attracts more than 40 000 people in about February every year, with approximately 12 000 of them actually swimming. Indeed it is the world's largest open-water swimming event. The race has been extended into a variety of races and whole families can compete.

The world-class and recently renovated **Kings Park Sporting Precinct** in Durban incorporates rugby and cricket stadia, athletics tracks, Kings Park, a cycling track, an archery range as well as restaurants, shops, children's play areas and a pedestrian walkway that links the complex to the beach.

The precinct also houses an Olympic-sized indoor swimming pool that hosts **Swimming World Cup** events, sometime from October to December each year, which draw top swimmers from across the globe. The annual **South African Senior National Aquatic Championships** are also held here, usually around April.

Kings Park Sporting Precinct is also home to the magnificent **Moses Mabhida Stadium**, built specially for the 2010 FIFA World Cup™ but designed as a multi-purpose venue and an amphitheatre, that can seat up to 70 000 people. An expansive 350-metre arch, complete with SkyCar, bisects the stadium and visitors can ascend to a viewing platform a staggering 106 metres above the field.

In July, domestic and international enthusiasts converge on Greyville Racecourse for the **Durban July**, the country's premier horse-racing event. Over that weekend the city hosts some 50 000 beautiful people, dressed to the nines, who come to revel in the excitement of the 2 200-metre sprint of the country's top thoroughbred horses.

As to be expected with such a conducive climate and warm sea, water sports play a big role in the lives of KZN residents and visitors. One of the major surf competitions is the **Mr Price Pro** held in June

The Golf Coast

About a fifth of South Africa's golf courses can be found in KZN. There are approximately 80 registered clubs in the province; some of the more popular ones include **Durban Country Club** (considered to be one of the best in the world) and its affiliated **Beachwood** course, the **Wild Coast Sun Country Club** just outside Port Edward, **Zimbali Country Club** in uMhlali, **Prince's Grant** in Dukuza, **Champagne Sports Resort** in the Central Drakensberg and **San Lameer Country Club** and **Selbourne Country Club** on the South Coast.

KZN's southern coastal region, once one of the best-kept secrets of South Africa's golfing circuit, has become increasingly popular – mainly because there are 11 golf courses within a radius of approximately 90 kilometres. Situated on the lush coastal strip, nine have the warm Indian Ocean as their backdrop. In recent years, most of them upgraded their facilities to keep up with international trends. The result is that this verdant stretch of coast, with its excellent accommodation and accompanying tourism amenities, is now popularly known as the Golf Coast.

While the Golf Coast is doing its utmost to ensure golfers a quality destination, other areas of the province are following suit. A number of investments have been made in golfing estates and facilities, such as the R1,8 billion Fairmont extension at Zimbali.

Because of the many great fantastic golf greens in the area, such as Southbroom Golf Course (below), the South Coast is often referred to as the Golf Coast by enthusiasts of the sport.

PLAYING GAMES

ABOVE: *The protected potato bass, which can weigh up to 110 kilograms, is one of the many wonderful creatures to be seen while diving in KZN waters.*

or July, once famously known as the Gunston 500. Well established since its conception in 1966, the competition attracts surfers and bikini-clad beauties, who flock from around the globe to participate in and support the event.

The more mainstream sports of **rugby**, **football** and **cricket** are huge in the province with regular provincial, national, international and friendly matches being played. There is little to beat the legendary KZN after-parties, where families braai and enjoy a few beers in the grounds after games.

The local rugby team, the **Sharks**, are particularly adored, and whenever a match is on supporters who don't make it to the stadium can be heard cheering from their homes or from sports bars around the city. Contact the Sharks Ticket Office (see contact list) for tickets. Otherwise, great places to watch games are **Joe Cool's** on Durban's beachfront, **Cool Runnings** with its big screen or alternatively one of the pubs along Florida Road.

ADVENTURE SPORTS
Diving

Aliwal Shoal at uMkomaas and Sodwana Bay, both beach launches, are known throughout the world as excellent dive sites. Year-round these locations offer a wealth of sea life to enjoy, but an added bonus is the annual sardine run that happens from about May to July.

During the run, more experienced divers have the opportunity of swimming with the huge shoals of sardines that move up the coast for winter, followed by game fish, sharks and dolphins. Both uMkomaas and Sodwana Bay have plenty of accommodation and quality dive operators.

For the adventurous, try a dive at Protea Banks off Shelley Beach, where Zambezi, tiger or hammerhead sharks may be seen. For those who would like a guaranteed dive with sharks, **uShaka Marine World** in Durban offers this experience in a controlled environment (see Beach and Sea p. 76).

Surfing

KZN has first-rate surf spots boasting consistently good swell and favourable wind conditions. There is also a variety of reef, point and beach breaks to suit all preferences, for both regular and goofy-footed riders. North Coast favourites include uMhlanga, Ballito and Salt Rock, while Green Point, St Michael's-on-Sea (St Mike's) and Lucien on the South Coast are popular.

Durban, sometimes called Surf City, has lots to offer. New Pier and Bay of Plenty on Durban's central beachfront are well loved and Cave Rock on the Bluff is notorious for its outstanding, sometimes dangerous surf. North Beach, Dairy Beach and Baggies are other good choices. There are plenty of surf schools to choose between.

The man-made wave at the **Wave House** at the Gateway Theatre of Shopping, uMhlanga, is excellent fun for adults, teenagers, and even younger children.

Kiteboarding, kayaking and whitewater rafting

Kiteboarding has attracted growing interest since its arrival in KZN, but it needs good levels of fitness and some skill. **Cyclone Extreme Products** hires out equipment and offers lessons on beaches suitable for beginners.

Jeep uShaka Surf and Adventure Centre offers sea-kayaking tours and kayak rentals from Durban beachfront, while **St Lucia Kayak Safaris** has tours in iSimangaliso Wetland Park. For any other paddling adventures, there are fabulous rivers and guided trails throughout the province.

Other water sports in KZN include **whitewater rafting**, which takes place in Oribi Gorge and the Central Drakensberg, and on the uThukela, Mkomazi and other rivers throughout the province. There is a variety of tour operators; for safety, ensure they are registered with the South African Rafting Association (SARA).

ABOVE: *On windy days, kiteboarders can be seen practising their skills on Durban's La Mercy Lagoon.*

ABOVE: *Gorge swinging at Oribi Gorge is one of the many activities on the South Coast for adventure junkies and nature lovers.*

ABOVE RIGHT: *Face your fears and explore KZN's beautiful forests on a canopy tour in Karkloof or the Drakensberg.*

Fishing

It takes a lot to beat fishing for tiger fish on the Pongola River and Jozini Dam or game fishing off KZN's coast. The North Coast is outstanding for rock and surf angling and freshwater fishing is available in dams in the Midlands and Drakensberg. Fly-fishing (both fresh and salt water) is also extremely popular. Numerous charter boats and splendid adventure guides are available to show visitors to best spots (see Beach and Sea p. 81).

Rock climbing, abseiling and mountaineering

The Drakensberg Mountains is the obvious place for high-peak mountaineering, rock climbing and hiking as it has some really fantastic buttresses, cliffs, waterfalls and gorges. There are also climbing sites at Mfolozi Crags, Kloof Gorge, Monteseel and Shongweni Resource Reserve.

Other high-level adventures include abseiling 107 metres off Howick Falls or 110 metres down alongside Lehr's Waterfall in Oribi Gorge, another of the world's highest commercial abseils. For a slightly more controlled climb, try the climbing wall at the Gateway Theatre of Shopping.

Fun alternatives are glides through forest canopies on foefie slides (zip lines) with **Karkloof Canopy Tours** or **Drakensberg Canopy Tour**, and a 100-metre swing across Oribi Gorge with **Wild 5**.

Ice climbing

For experienced rock climbers, the uKhahlamba-Drakensberg Park offers some fantastic ice climbing – a great introduction to the world of alpine climbing. Two- and three-day courses are available during the winter months that include food, transport, guiding and permits. Contact **Peak High Mountaineering** for details (see contact list).

Three good areas for ice climbing are Sani Pass, for short, easy and sheltered climbs; Rhino Peak, known for its snow gulley routes; and Giant's Castle, which has the longest and possibly best routes in the country.

Mountain biking

The Midlands, because of its aesthetics and gently rolling hills, is a popular mountain biking location; indeed for those who enjoy nice gentle rides there are mountain bike trails all over KZN. Lotheni in the uKhahlamba-Drakensberg Park has an 8-kilometre mountain bike trail where cyclists can stop and swim and see the historical Gelib Tree site, and Oribi Gorge, a few kilometres inland from Port Shepstone on the South Coast, has some rewarding trails too.

Flying

Looking down onto the fragile earth from up in the sky can be a life-changing experience and is always breathtaking. While learning to fly can be expensive, KZN offers some of the best instruction at various venues, such as **Zero Four Flight School** at Margate Airport as well as other good ones at Virginia Airport in Durban.

Those who would like to fly without committing to a course can take a flip in a light aircraft, or go up in a helicopter. There are numerous places where this is possible. Durban has at least five operators, including **Air Safaris** while **South Coast Helicopter Services** operates on the South Coast in season, and on the North Coast there is **JNC Helicopter Tours**. For tours in other areas, **Beach and Bush** has some lovely options.

To get even closer to nature, **microlighting** is wonderful option. If that still doesn't get the pulse going, just leap out a plane with a parachute. This can be done with an instructor in a tandem jump with **Skydive Durban** from Pietermaritzburg Airport and **Blue Sky** at Cato Ridge Airfield.

Paragliding takes some skill and training, but tandem flights with an instructor are also available for beginners, with **Skyguide Paragliding** in Westville and with **Blue Sky**.

A bit of pampering

If sport and adventure activities are not your thing, why not relax in a spa and get pampered while your other half gets his or her adrenaline fix? **Fardoun Spa** in Nottingham Road has skilled masseurs, Reiki and bioenergy specialists, a traditional African healer and highly trained aestheticians. There is also a couples' treatment suite with a hydrotherapy bath if your partner wants to join you to relieve tired, stiff muscles after his or her adventure activity of choice.

Another exciting option is the expansive eco-friendly **Karkloof Spa Wellness & Wildlife Retreat** in Cramond, set on a 3 500-hectare game reserve. Along with an array of spa treatments, facilities offered include a manicure/pedicure lounge, flotation pool, open-air Jacuzzi, as well as Kneipp therapy pools and sauna and steam rooms.

The outside bathrooms at Kosi Forest Lodge provide a relaxing respite.

ABOVE: *A helicopter flip provides a new perspective on the world below.*

6

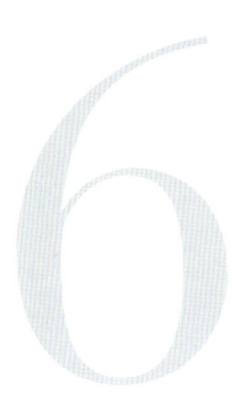

FOOD AND DRINK

Records from Portuguese explorers who sailed along KZN shores show that Durban and the surrounding region have long provided nourishment for travellers. Today, the province still has a reputation for providing excellent food, especially in the way of curries.

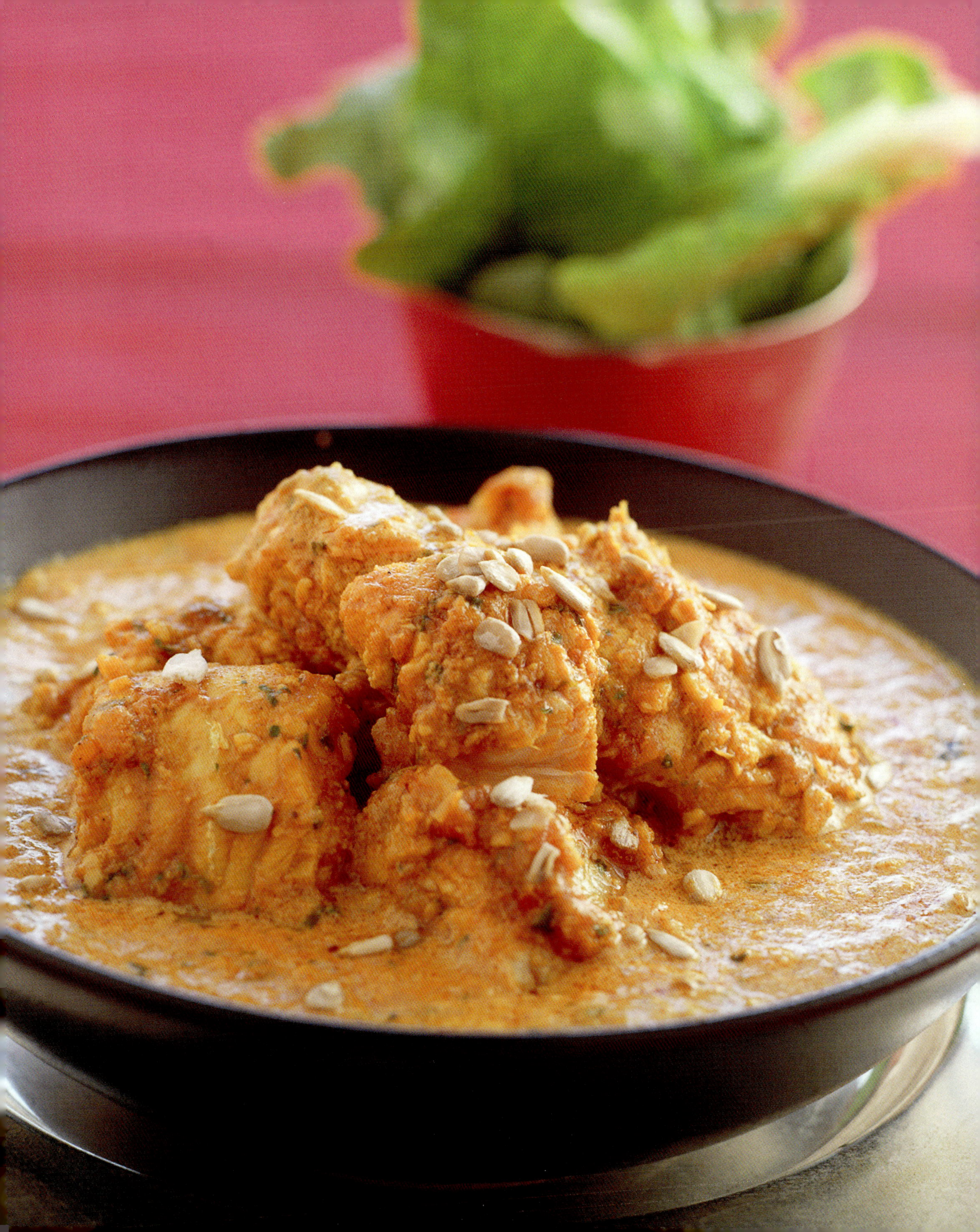

FOOD AND DRINK

PREVIOUS PAGE: *KZN has a reputation for having the best curry in the country.*

BELOW: *The heady smells of aromatic spices are a constant reminder of KZN's Indian heritage.*

BELOW RIGHT: *Bunny chows, filled with steaming curry, are one of the province's great takeaway food inventions.*

GOOD FARE
Curry kings

Due to the strong Indian presence, KZN is well known for its excellent Indian cuisine. A good rule of thumb is to eat curry in a place where there is a large Indian clientele. The **Britannia Hotel**, situated under the flyover crossing the Mgeni River, is always full of friendly Indian folk, especially at Friday lunchtime.

For a more upmarket experience, try **Ulundi** at the Royal Hotel, which specialises in *thali* – small bowls of curry and condiments served on traditional brass Indian trays. The **Copper Chimney** on Durban's beachfront serves an extremely good, reasonably priced Halaal curry.

Jewel of India at the Southern Sun Elangeni hotel has a great selection of vegetarian food, otherwise focusing on north Indian food, which although just as spicy tends to be less hot and somewhat creamier than southern Indian dishes.

Little India and **Palki**, both in Musgrave Road, are great for family outings. They both serve the famous *masala dosha*, a large, thin, rice-flour pancake rolled around a ball of potato curry.

Taj Mahal and **Indian Summer** are both good options in Durban North. For starters at the latter try the *chaat*, snacks as sold on Mumbai's beachfront, before moving on to prawn curry.

Takeaways are always reasonably priced, but check first to see whether the curry is 'extremely hot' or just 'very hot'. A celebrated takeaway speciality is the fabulous Durban **bunny chow** – a hollowed-out half-loaf of fresh bread filled with steaming hot curry.

Spoilt for choice

KZN has a number of excellent restaurants with outstanding chefs. **Mo's** on Durban's Florida Road is *the* place to eat prawn-and-coconut soup and other yummy Thai-style noodle dishes. Another restaurant close by in Morningside is **Spice**, highly rated for its imaginative lunch specials and wonderfully warm vibe.

Berea's **Café 1999** can be noisy, but has a great menu and excellent wines. For an interesting venue as well as really good food, an old favourite is the **Roma Revolving Restaurant**, where views over the whole of Durban city complement the Italian specialities and serious dessert trolley.

Out in the suburbs, Hillcrest's **Aubergine & Andreotti's** has a highly rated cosmopolitan menu. The seasonal specials change continually, so it is worth returning frequently. uMhlanga Rocks, to the south of the city, is home to one of KZN's best-known restaurants, **Ile Maurice**, which serves outstanding seafood in a colonial atmosphere.

ABOVE: *A meal in The Grill Room of the beautiful Oyster Box Hotel in uMhlanga Rocks is fine dining at its best.*

FOOD AND DRINK

BELOW: *What better way to wash down the delicious food along the Midlands Meander than by stopping for a pint at the Nottingham Road Brewery at the Rawdons Hotel?*

BELOW RIGHT: *Foodies love rambling along the Midlands Meander, finding specialities such as the olives at Romesco Olives in Howick.*

The **Waffle House** in Ramsgate on the South Coast is a real institution among locals and regular visitors. As its name suggests, it offers delicious Belgian waffles, and really should not be missed.

Another option is a banana farm tour on the far South Coast near Port Edward followed by a light lunch at the **Banana Café and Pancake House**.

On the North Coast head for **Zimbali Lodge**, a stylish restaurant in an Indonesian setting with great views over the golf greens and sea.

Also good is **Umami** at Ballito. The food is excellent and the views over the deck, pool and wetland forest are spectacular.

Food meander

A wonderfully laid-back way to spend a weekend is to take a slow drive on the Midlands Meander. Although the Meander has long been associated with arts and crafts, it is fast becoming one of KZN's great foodie destinations. A good place to buy some *padkos* to eat in the car, or to get a picnic basket for an alfresco lunch, is the **Hilton Farm Stall**, where you can find delicious smoked trout, fresh farm fruit and vegetables, pickles, jams and preserves, cheeses and warm homemade breads.

A family favourite near Howick is **Peel's Honey Shop** – home of raw honey, creamed honey and

FOOD AND DRINK

many delicious types of honey-based confectionery made from the distinctive honey from the Mist Belt, such as peanut-and-sesame brittle.

At Howick find **The Grapevine** deli with its yummy pies, fresh salads and sarmies, delicious cakes and tarts and range of pickles, jams and other home-made food items.

Granny Mouse Country House & Spa at Lidgetton is synonymous with fabulous food, an award-winning menu and outstanding wine cellar, while **Günther's**, overlooking the gorgeous Caversham Valley, is the place for authentic sauerkraut and German and Swiss sausages.

Caversham Mill Restaurant at Balgowan is seriously popular, not just because of its good, wholesome food, affordable prices and friendly service, but also for its setting on the site of an original 1857 mill that overlooks a little waterfall on the banks of the Lions River.

Swissland Cheese is also in Balgowan. Apart from the amazing prize-winning, ash-coated Drakensberg Brie, try the other goat's milk cheeses made on the farm, such as the Chevin, smoked Chevin or white-mould St Maure. They also prepare picnic packs to enjoy outside, and kids will love watching the milking and feeding the goats.

BELOW LEFT: *Coffee lovers should keep an eye open for Bean Green coffee.*

BELOW: *Another tantalising local product not to be missed by more adventurous foodies is home-brewed Zulu beer.*

ABOVE: *The Hilton Farm Stall at The Rotunda sells a whole range of home-baked goodies and other fresh produce.*

Dargle Valley Pork is the best, some say the only, place for smoked bacon, pork chipolata sausages and other pork goodies – as well as some fine free-range lamb – all of which are hormone-free.

Nottingham Road has a number of famous hotels and pubs. Famed for its delicious croissants, breads and home-made pastries rather than its duck, **The Whistling Duck** is also great for healthy comfort food such as soups and lasagnes. Don't miss the Portuguese *pastéis de nata*. **Café Bloom** is between 'Notties' and Rosetta. The lovely garden café serves stunning gingerbread muffins with farmhouse butter, and has other wonderful baked goods as well as great breakfasts.

The Wine Cellar in Rosetta is rumoured to have one of the largest cellars in KZN. Choose one of some 2 500 labels to go with your pre-booked cheese platter or picnic basket, which can be enjoyed on the banks of the river. Another excellent cheese shop nearby is at the **Marrakesh Cheese Farm**, which produces some 15 different Mediterranean-styled cheeses, some blended from goat's and cow's milk and some from pure goat's milk. Well known for its 14-month matured Midlands Reserve Parmesan, the farm's Pecorino and red-onion cream cheese are also delicious.

Between Nottingham Road and Rosetta, watch ice cream being manufactured, learn about ice cream and, most important of all, eat ice cream and other yummy ice-cream-based products at the **Mad About Cows** ice-cream farm.

Another good stop is Rosetta's **Horizons Gourmet Picnics**, where meanderers can relax with their picnic basket on the lawn on blankets and pillows (or at dapper little tables) while looking out over the mountains as the children play.

Another excellent award-winning restaurant found in an elegant, historic boutique hotel is

Hartford House in Mooi River, which offers top-of-the-range cuisine. Lunch is a stunning à la carte menu while dinner is a five-course meal, changing daily.

Richard Poynton, chef and owner of **Cleopatra Mountain Farmhouse**, has received much acclaim for his innovative and fresh menu. He travelled the world training with top chefs, and spends great effort tracking down exotic ingredients that he prepares with fresh produce straight out of his kitchen garden. It is essential to book at this award-winning restaurant, located on the very edge of the uKhahlamba-Drakensberg Park. Diners are usually so satiated after an exquisite six-course meal that they want to stay overnight.

Fresh food markets

The best places to buy the freshest food would of course be at the farm of origin. While many farms have kiosks that sell their fresh produce directly to the public, another great way to buy fresh food is at the fresh food and produce markets that are held in many towns and villages.

Fresh produce or farmers' markets have become quite the rage with foodies, and just about every region in the province holds them monthly, if not weekly. Most items sold are made, grown or produced locally, or at the very least come from other farming districts around the country. Traditionally, markets start at daybreak, getting busy around 09:00. While some close at 11:00, others stay open until 14:00 or so. A jaunt to these markets is a wonderful way to spend a morning, and besides shopping, visitors can enjoy breakfast, drink coffee and watch people at the same time as supporting local farmers and crafters.

The weekly Saturday-morning **Shongweni Farmers' Market** in Assagay is said to be the best

ABOVE LEFT: *Freshly roasted coffee can be purchased at places such as Terbodore Coffee Roasters in Curry's Post.*

ABOVE: *The Marrakesh Cheese Farm in Rosetta produces a delicious array of fresh cheese.*

FOOD AND DRINK

farmers' market in KZN, an opinion that is supported by the various awards it has won and the continued support of marketgoers from around the area. Many locals buy their weekly groceries here while taking the opportunity to socialise and catch up with their friends over breakfast and steamy farm coffee as the sun rises.

Various wonderful food products are available, including delicious home-smoked bacon, organic chicken, veggies and herbs, fresh strawberries, farm cheeses, flowers, home-baked goodies, biltong, Madagascan vanilla, olive oil, pickles and preserves, wine, treats for dogs and much more.

The continually growing craft section offers a wide variety of items that are bound to satisfy creative and practical requirements, such as furniture, sculptures, jewellery and clothing.

A festive supplement is the Christmas Night Market, held in mid-December each year.

The Saturday **Pietermaritzburg Farmers' Market** has a wide variety of produce for sale, including plants, herbs and flowers, organically grown vegetables, fresh eggs, baked goods, farm coffee, fresh home-made samoosas and vetkoeke and other culinary delights. Have a Chinese take-away breakfast or enjoy a great greasy breakfast on a bun while listening to the town crier calling out the weekly specials.

A real foodie find is the **Karkloof Farmers' Market**, just outside of Howick every Saturday morning, which showcases a fabulous selection of locally grown and made produce. Marketgoers can buy honey, cheese, salads, veggies and a variety of breads and other delicious baked goods, as well as pickles, jams and fresh juices. The Moroccan food stall, with its exotic North African flavours, is particularly popular.

There are several markets in Durban too. Get to the daily **Victoria Street Fish Market** on Bertha Mkhize Street (former Victoria Street) early for the freshest fish straight off the boats. Another market worth an early start to secure the best-quality produce is the nearby **Early Morning Market** on Julius Nyerere Avenue (former Warwick Avenue), which runs from Monday to Thursday, although there are rumours of this having to move to make way for a mall. The excitement tends to die down later in the day, but it is still fascinating to visit.

The **Gordon Road Fresh Food Market** takes place at Gordon Road Girls' School in Greyville on Saturday mornings.

ALCOHOL
Wine

The Stables Wine Estate is located on an old stud farm outside Nottingham Road. It produces a range of wines, and has won several awards and accolades. Look out for the Sharks range – Raggie Red, Zambezi Pink and Silver Tip – as well as the Springbok Rugby World Cup commemorative wine. Another popular wine is the Prince Imperial.

Due to the soils, climate, and structure of the fruit at harvest, Stables wines have unique characteristics and are very different from Cape wines. They are generally lower in alcohol, dry and fruity, having been aged lightly in French oak barrels.

The Stables Wine Estate holds a number of fun festivals throughout the year. As these change, the best thing to do is to call them for details prior to visiting (see contact list).

Traditional Zulu beer

In Zulu society, women are the brewers of traditional beer. Making *utshwala besintu* or *umqombothi*, as traditional Zulu beer is called, begins with soaking maize or sorghum in water. Once the grains start germinating, they are washed and dried.

They are then ground to produce a fairly rough powder. This is cooked like porridge in a pot of water over a fire, after which the mixture is left in big beer pots to cool for a few days.

Finally malt is poured on top and the mixture is covered to keep it warm while it ferments. This last step takes anything up to five days, but in warm weather the beer can be ready within three.

The beer is strained through woven grass strainers made especially for the purpose. Traditionally beer is served in clay pots (see Creative Thinking p. 45). Zulu beer is not always considered an alcoholic beverage as it has a low alcohol content when fresh. However, the longer it is left to ferment, the stronger the brew. Many Zulu women develop a reputation for their beer-making skills, and in their households there is seldom a shortage of helping hands.

Opportunities to taste *utshwala* are possible at any traditional ceremony, cultural village, shebeen or tavern. If in doubt, ask a local.

Ilala palm wine

On the other hand, tapping ilala wine is traditionally a man's job. Ilala palm wine, known as *ubusulu*,

ABOVE: *The Abingdon Wine Estate near Lions River has several cultivars, including Cabernet Sauvignon, Syrah, Sauvignon Blanc, Viognier and Chardonnay.*

CHAPTER ONE
Like all Robson's beer, this was handcrafted
only the finest malted barley, hops, water and
yeast. Inspired by South Africa, our
EAST COAST ALE
blends citrus aromas and fine hop
to make a really refreshing beer that
in colour. It's best enjoyed with friends
That's how we like it, anyway.
you might imagine that you can
glimpse of the Indian Ocean
the green hills that surround
Shongweni Brewery.
ROBSON'S
CHAPTER ONE
EAST COAST ALE
ROBSON'S
70513

is restricted to areas such as Maputaland, in northeastern KZN, and southern Mozambique, where ilala palms grow in the wild. Although the industry is growing, tapping sap is extremely labour-intensive and ultimately provides a mere subsistence income for individual tappers. The current price for a five-litre container of freshly tapped Ilala palm sap is in the region of R15. A limiting factor is that the price is set by the local tribal authority to ensure that it remains affordable to most of the community.

Ilala trees are owned by a particular household. A healthy clump of ilala plants are burnt to rid them of their spiked leaves and to concentrate the sap. The stem is trimmed and either a funnel-shaped leaf is inserted into a hole or a V-shape is cut into the stem, down which sap drips into a container. The plant is trimmed two or three times a day over a period of five to seven weeks.

Ilala wine is alcoholic from the start, although like Zulu beer it becomes stronger the longer it is left. The Tembe-Tsonga people are famous for their wine making, but be warned, it is an acquired taste. It looks like litchi juice and seems sweet and refreshing when it is still fresh – but it should at all times be approached with caution! Ask staff at local lodges in the area for some help finding some ilala wine-sipping opportunities.

Beer

KZN has a very enjoyable **Brew Route** and one of the most modern commercial breweries in the Southern Hemisphere. **South African Breweries Ltd** is the South African arm of SAB Miller and the second largest brewer in the world. As you can imagine, tours around the massive brewery in Prospecton West are extremely popular.

The two other large commercial brewers offering interesting tours are the **Congella United National Breweries Ltd** in Durban and the **Ijuba United National Breweries Ltd** in Dundee. Both of these brewers produce traditional beer or *umqombothi* commercially, making it both accessible and affordable to a large spectrum of the market. Various flavours such as banana, vanilla and chocolate have been introduced and are now being exported throughout Africa. The tours also provide an insight into apartheid beer laws and inevitably end with a festive and thoroughly enjoyable beer tasting with snacks.

There are great microbreweries in the area too. The **Nottingham Road Brewery** at the Rawdons Hotel in the Midlands produces some 20 000 litres a month and distributes nationally. The hotel is a good place to eat as well as taste some of the silly-named beers, such as the Tiddly Toad and Pye-Eyed Possum. The **Zululand Brewing Company** in eShowe produces good beers, some of which are flavoured, and the **Shongweni Brewery** outside Hillcrest has its own unique range.

While not a brewery, a great place to enjoy a Polish Okocim beer in the Midlands is the **Little Poland Restaurant and Pub**, which also makes its own Polish sausages.

OPPOSITE: *KZN is lucky to have several microbreweries, and wholesome local beer, such as the Shongweni Brewery's Robson's, is readily enjoyed.*

BEACH AND SEA

KZN's coastline stretches
from the Mtamvuna River
on the Eastern Cape border
in the south to Kosi Bay
on the Mozambican border
in the north. This tropical
560-kilometre coastline, with
its many bays and sandy
beaches, provides endless fun,
water-related activities.

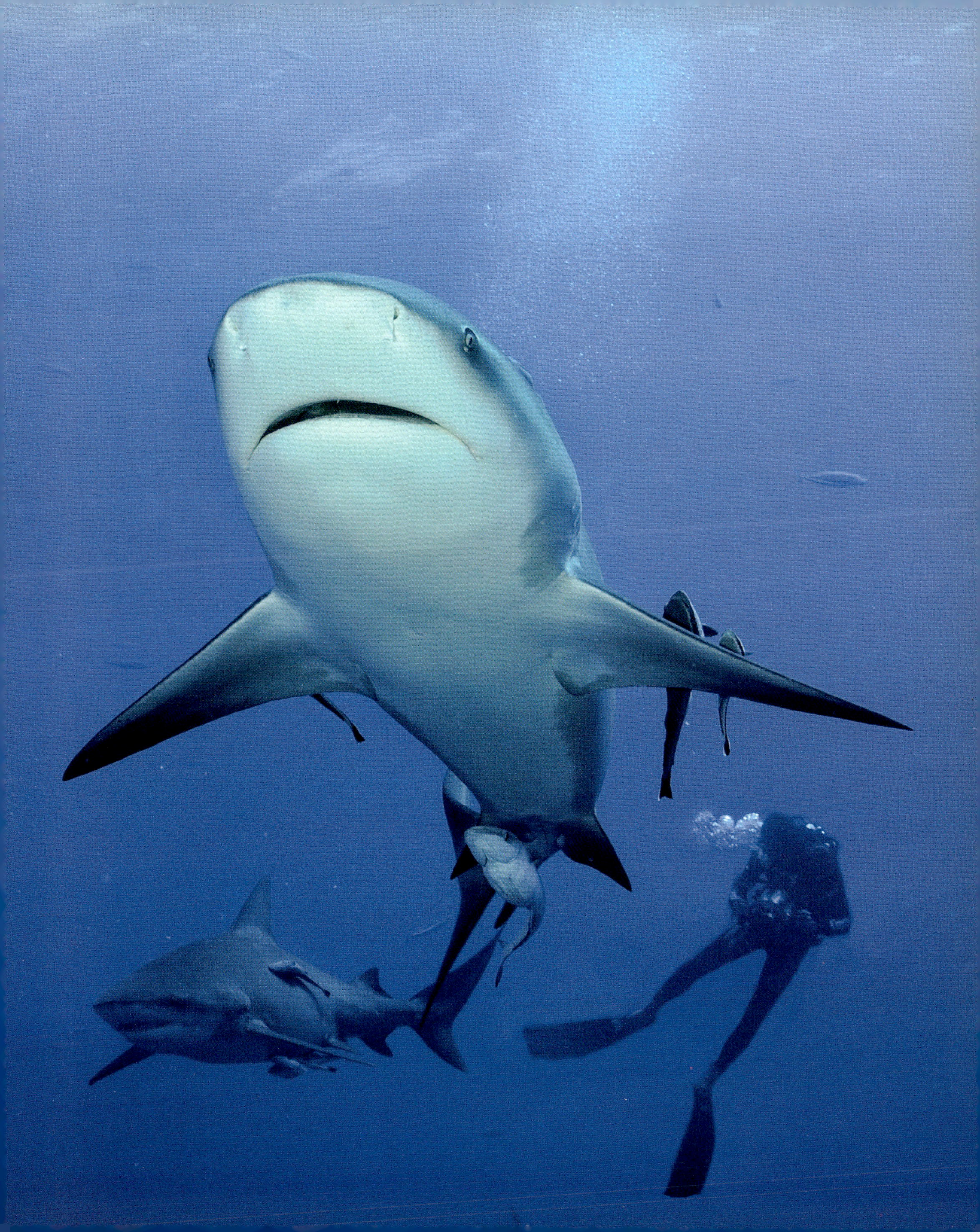

BEACH AND SEA

PREVIOUS PAGE: *For the courageous, diving with sharks, such as the bull or Zambezi shark, can be an exhilarating experience.*

BELOW: *Southbroom, on the South Coast, has unspoilt, long, sandy, white beaches.*

> ### Lifeguards
>
> KZN is lucky to have professionally trained lifeguards to assist bathers. Both the North and South coasts of KZN offer great swimming, but the conditions can be unpredictable. Where possible, swim only at lifeguarded beaches when lifeguards are on duty, listen to their instructions and follow the beach rules.

BEACHES

Beach tourism worldwide is a growing holiday option. KZN, with its fabulous climate, sandy beaches and warm Indian Ocean, offers the most significant beach attraction in the country, for both foreign and domestic tourists. Average water temperature is 24 °C, and it rarely drops below 17 °C. There are some terrific beaches all along the coast. Both the North and South coasts' beaches are famous for their beauty, warm water, safe bathing and great fishing opportunities.

South Coast

Port Edward, just north of the border with the Eastern Cape, is not only great for swimming, but is also popular for fishing off the rocks and whale watching, during season. Heading north up the coast, **Leisure Bay** is a lovely, quiet beach, but it has no facilities, so go prepared. The swimming is great and the rocks are easy for children to clamber on. Lifeguards are on duty in season at both of these beaches as well as at **Trafalgar Beach**, which has good surfing and borders the northern edge of the **Trafalgar Marine Reserve**, administered by **Ezemvelo KZN Wildlife**.

Marina Beach and the beach at the luxury private golf resort of **San Lameer** are also good spots, as is **Ramsgate**. **Margate Beach**, a little north of Ramsgate, is a popular domestic holiday destination. In fact it is one of the busiest places on the South Coast, especially during season, and has plenty of facilities.

The pretty beach of St Michael's-on-Sea, known as **St Mike's** by the locals, is safe for swimming and has good facilities. Due to its commercial nature, it can get quite busy in holiday seasons. Just north of Port Shepstone, **uMtentwini**, **Sea Park** and **Southport** are all popular family beaches with the added advantage of good fishing and, depending on tides and winds, they are excellent surf spots.

The **Pumula Beach Hotel** is extremely popular as a family holiday destination as it has superb facilities for children. It also has a conference centre. But it is the picturesque **uMzumbe Beach**, onto which the hotel looks, that is the real draw card. **Stebel Rocks**, on the southern end of the beach, is outstanding for angling. There is a little tidal pool and it is also safe to swim in the sea. The surf is great, and one of the biggest 'black' surf clubs in the country is based here, where many up-and-coming black surfers are 'finding their feet' on the waves.

The lovely small beach of **Hibberdene** is a perfect holiday spot with ski-boat launch facilities. **Bazley** is another firm family favourite. The nearby award-winning **MacNicol's Bazley Beach Caravan & Camping Resort** overlooks the lagoon and beach. The swimming beach is popular and lifeguards are on duty during season. Angling off the rocks is also rewarding. **Pennington's** little beach – another much-loved angling spot – is close to the **uMdoni Park Golf Course Club** and can be accessed via a short walk through a patch of coastal forest.

Scottburgh Main Beach is often used for surf and windsurfing contests. Pedal boats are for hire on the lagoon and the grassy banks are great for picnics. The area caters to all age groups, from children to the elderly and there are restaurants, shops and toilets nearby. **Scottburgh South Beach** is much quieter and more suited to angling and snorkelling than swimming.

Durban

Durban is celebrated for its safe swimming, shark nets, lifeguards and great facilities. The 6-kilometre-long stretch of beachfront promenade, famously known as the Golden Mile before it expanded,

ABOVE: *The safe beaches and good facilities on the South Coast, at places such as Margate, draw both local and international holiday-makers.*

BEACH AND SEA

has always been one of the city's premier tourist attractions. An early-morning or late-afternoon walk along the promenade is a favourite for many residents. Strollers can stop for coffee at a beachside café or watch the surfers, joggers, skateboarders and fishermen from the many piers jutting out to sea. There may even be a traditional African baptism to observe. For a ride, flamboyant rickshas pulled by elaborately dressed Zulu men may be hired.

Southern Durban beaches include **uShaka** – good for snorkelling and diving. It is a kind of nursery area for new surfers as the waves are smaller, making them ideal for beginners. It is also where nipper (junior lifesaving) training takes place.

uShaka is situated in front of the **uShaka Marine World** complex, made up of several sections. **uShaka Sea World** houses an aquarium, dolphinarium, a seal pool and a penguin rookery. **uShaka Wet 'n Wild** has freshwater swimming pools for adults and children as well as a variety of fun water slides, ranging from tame to gut-wrenching in intensity.

When hunger strikes, there are several fast-food outlets and restaurants to choose from. Try **Moyo uShaka Pier** for a fantasy African beach experience. It is situated along the **uShaka Village Walk**, a marine-themed shopping area that has retail outlets and several other good eateries. Another tasty option is the **Cargo Hold**, for a spicy, fruity and exotic menu that uses KZN's freshest local produce. It is located inside the **Phantom Ship**, the life-sized, 1920s-era cargo steamer that is the centrepiece

BELOW: *The beach at picturesque uMhlanga Rocks, which is good for swimming, is lined with holiday homes and hotels.*

of the complex. While eating, diners can watch massive sharks swim about in the marine shark tank that acts as a backdrop to the restaurant.

uShaka is followed by **Addington**, **South Beach** and **New Beach**. The promenade along New Beach, once known as Wedge, has been widened and extended, expanding the link between the South and North Durban beaches and allowing for more movement between them. The surrounding facilities have been upgraded, and New Beach is also now connected by a walkway to the Moses Mabhida Stadium, allowing spectators to move directly between the two places.

The central beaches are usually busier with **Dairy**, **North Beach**, **Bay of Plenty** and **Snake Park** being popular for surfing and swimming, and angling takes place off permitted piers.

Attractions in the central section are established bar-cum-restaurants **Joe Cool's** and **The Deck**, **Minitown**, a miniature reconstruction of Durban, and the **Amphitheatre Gardens**, home to popular children's paddling pools. There is also the saltwater **Rachel Finlayson Pool**, open year-round. The whole area underwent massive renovation for the 2010 FIFA World Cup™, creating opportunities for new businesses and restaurants.

The northern section has **Battery Beach**, opposite the old Natal Command army base, and **Suncoast Casino & Entertainment World** has green lawns rolling down to **Suncoast Beach**. The hotel complex is complete with restaurants, amphitheatre, gambling halls and movie theatres. **eThekwini** attracts kiteboarders and **Blue Lagoon**, by the Mgeni River mouth, is popular with birdwatchers and nature lovers. It is also where the beachfront stretch comes to an end.

North Coast

Moving up the North Coast, the first good swimming beach is at **uMhlanga**, a picturesque and busy resort town. There is a narrow, winding promenade that follows the edge of the beach, and the pier leading down to its iconic lighthouse is sculptured to look like a whale's ribcage.

ABOVE: *Once a small fishing village, Ballito has grown into a large holiday town due to its popular beaches.*

BEACH AND SEA

Next comes **uMdloti**, which is popular for its safe swimming and productive fishing. It also has great waves, which are good for surfing and kiteboarding, when the wind is right. uMdloti village has some fantastic restaurants overlooking the beaches and the sea. There are lifeguards at both uMhlanga and uMdloti.

North of the town, in more rural areas, are **Thompson's Bay**, **Salmon Bay** and Ballito's beaches, **Clarke Bay** and **Willards Beach.** These are well loved but quieter beaches. Thompson's Bay has steep access steps, making it difficult for the elderly, while Salmon Bay is more accessible. As it is a ski-boat launch site there are no shark nets, so swimmers should not venture too far out. Shark nets are provided at both Clarke Bay and Willards Beach, and lifeguards are also on duty. There are fantastic surf spots near these beaches, and a tidal pool can be found a little south of Clarke Bay.

Sheffield Beach has everything a beach should have – rock pools for snorkelling and for children to play in, great fishing and good diving. Enjoy a picnic there or take a stroll to **Christmas Bay** further along the beach.

Zinkwazi means 'place of the fish eagles' – an apt name for this beach where these magnificent birds can often be heard. The beach and its surrounding indigenous forest and lagoon are frequented by locals and holiday-makers alike. Families enjoy trips on the lagoon, water sports, fishing, canoeing and ski-boat fishing, although caution must be taken when swimming as there are no shark nets.

Mtunzini offers surf angling and expansive beaches, and children enjoy frolicking in the lagoon with its pretty fringe of mangroves. Take care not to swim when the water is brown, which happens after heavy rains. The nearby raffia palm plantation, where the palms stretch skywards some 16 metres, is a national heritage site. There are also a nine-hole golf course at the **Mtunzini Country Club**, which is close by.

A major highlight of the North Coast is of course **iSimangaliso Wetland Park**, which is the province's first World Heritage Site. It boasts magnificent, unspoilt beaches. Just off Cape Vidal is **Mission Rocks**, where the strangely pocked, eroded rocks create shelter for pleasant picnic spots. **Bat's Cave**, a short walk northwards, and **Perrier's Rocks**, to the south, are both good for angling.

Visitors to Cape Vidal over any major holiday must arrive early as only a set number of cars are

BELOW: *The quiet and unspoilt beaches of Cape Vidal are one of the many reasons iSimangaliso Wetland Park was declared a World Heritage Site.*

permitted entry. Out of season, though, lucky visitors may have this pristine beach, with its long stretches of sand, excellent snorkelling and warm water, all to themselves. It is also a ski-boat launch site and is popular with deep-sea and spear fishermen alike.

Mr Price Pro

Originally known as the Gunston 500, the Mr Price Pro is one of the longest-running surf competitions in the world, drawing top surfers from around the globe.

Running parallel to the Mr Price Pro are beach soccer and volleyball events, body boarding and Jet Ski competitions as well as other fun water sport activities.

Sodwana Bay has fantastic fishing and diving, and experienced divers may be able to see the prehistoric coelacanth.

Rocktail Beach Camp is in the coastal forest reserve in the northern section of the park, about half a kilometre from **Island Rock Beach**, which is an outstanding offshore dive spot. Just up the beach, **Lala Nek** is a great snorkelling and excellent swimming beach, with hardly a soul to be seen. Safe, uninhabited beaches like these are a rarity in the world today, and should be enjoyed with the utmost respect.

Kosi Bay has great fishing and snorkelling, and its four lakes, packed with crocodiles and hippos, offer exciting game viewing.

The park has several other noteworthy beaches, with an array of accommodation and various activities on offer (see World Heritage Wetland pp. 111–13).

ABOVE: *Hippos wallow in the St Lucia Estuary in iSimangaliso Wetland Park, while fishermen try to catch something for the braai.*

ABOVE: *Fishing off the piers, such as this one at Margate, is a popular and rewarding pastime.*

OPPOSITE: *Durban's harbour mouth is the gateway to this busy port.*

ACTIVITIES
Surfing and sea kayaking

Durban is famous throughout the world for its waves, not just for the major world qualifiers and competitions they bring but also for fun, recreational surfing. There are a number of outstanding surf schools in the area with highly qualified instructors, so wannabe surfers can learn how to ride the waves.

Off many of KZN's main beaches people can be seen paddling about or fishing from their paddle skis or sea kayaks. A great way to explore the ocean is to do a short course and take a sea safari. They are usually run out of Durban, but depending on the operator may go as far as Mozambique (see Playing Games p. 57).

Windsurfing and kiteboading

There is a sufficient amount of wind for both windsurfing and kiteboarding along the KZN coast. Kiteboarding takes some energy and skill, but there

> ### The Southern African Sustainable Seafood Initiative
>
> With global overfishing a serious reality, 80% of commercial fish stocks have been overfished or are at maximum levels, and certain local fish species are also rare. At the same time, the demand for seafood is growing. The **World Wide Fund For Nature South Africa** (WWF–SA) initiated the Southern African Sustainable Seafood Initiative (SASSI), the first campaign of its kind in Africa.
>
> SASSI has created the **Consumers' Species List**, available on the SASSI website, to help the public make informed choices regarding the seafood that they eat. For instant advice on the move, SMS the species name to SASSI's FishMS number (see contact list).

80

BEACH AND SEA

Commercial harbours

The **Port of Durban** is the busiest in Southern Africa, operating 24 hours a day year-round and handling some 4 500 sea-going vessels and 75 million tonnes of cargo annually. Apart from cargo ships, various cruise liners and pleasure boats make use of Durban's harbour. The entrance channel is 19 metres deep, shallowing to 16 metres inside the harbour.

Initially built for the export of coal, the **Port of Richards Bay** is South Africa's premier bulk port. It handles some 1 750 ships and more than 82 million tonnes of cargo per year. The two harbours account for about 78% of the country's cargo tonnage.

---

are lessons available at most major centres, and there are beaches set aside for these pursuits.

Fishing

Three kinds of fishing take place in the province – commercial, subsistence and recreational, which includes collecting bait and rock seafood. Rules and regulations govern each activity and all of them require a permit. These can be obtained either from Ezemvelo KZN Wildlife or from post offices countrywide.

There are many excellent rock and shore angling spots along the coast that are used by rock and surf anglers on a regular basis, while deep-sea fishing can be enjoyed from any of the many charter boats.

The Maputaland coastline is well known for its large variety of tropical reefs and pelagic fish and is home to the southernmost coral reefs in the world. However, fishing is restricted, and in some cases even prohibited. But despite this there are still some wonderful legal angling spots; heading south from the border there are Cape Vidal, St Lucia, Maphelane, Richards Bay and uThukela River mouth. On the other side of Durban, try Green Point near uMkomaas, Rocky Bay near Pennington, Stebel Rocks at uMzumbe or the rocks near Port Shepstone's Mzimkhulu River mouth (see Playing Games p. 58).

Ski boats can be chartered at many launch sites along the coast or out of Durban. Depending on the season, and whether one is going for trawling for game fish or bottom fishing, the chances of catching dorado, barracuda, marlin or even the odd shark are good, but obviously catches cannot be guaranteed.

Cool Runnings Fishing Charters, with its trademark reggae music, is a fun, easy-going option. All gear is provided and food and beverages may be included if desired. The operation also runs cruises offshore Durban and around the harbour, stopping at **Wilson's Wharf** for a plate of oysters.

Lynski is one of the oldest charter operators with many years of experience and a good reputation, while **Hakuna Matata Charters** offers luxurious 58-foot catamarans for private cruises, at a somewhat higher cost.

BEACH AND SEA

MARINE ENVIRONMENT

Due to its long management and conservation history, KZN's marine environment is incredibly rich in biodiversity. There are three marine protected areas in the province.

iSimangaliso Wetland Park incorporates some 220 kilometres of the North Coast and protects coral, coelacanths and sea turtles, among other marine life. The small **Trafalgar Marine Reserve** on the South Coast conserves 100-million-year-old intertidal fossils, invertebrate resources and subtidal seaweeds. The third marine reserve is **Aliwal Shoal**, off the South Coast town of uMkomaas. It is 20,6 kilometres long and 5 kilometres wide, and includes a submerged reef supporting a rich mixture of tropical and subtropical species.

KZN's marine environment is divided into two distinct regions, one north of St Lucia Estuary, within iSimangaliso Wetland Park, the other south of it. Evidence of this division was found in exciting research into intertidal ecology, subtidal seaweed biology and oceanography.

The nutrient-poor Agulhas Current flows at speeds of some 3–5 metres per second along Maputaland's northern coastline, making it one of the fastest currents on earth. This section of the coast runs almost exactly north–south in a straight line. The continental shelf is also very narrow, only 1–3 kilometres in some places, and a number of parallel submarine canyons lie along the shelf break offshore. Few rivers flow into the sea along this stretch, but it is believed that many of the submarine canyons could have been cut by ancient rivers.

Sand and other soft sediments dominate the coastal and subtidal habitats, although rocky outcrops lie along the coastline at 5–10-kilometre intervals and some subtidal coral and rock reefs do occur. South of Cape Vidal, the coastline takes a turn inland and the continental shelf expands out to sea. This expansion is known as the Natal Bight and it pushes the centre of the Agulhas Current further away from the shore, creating an upwelling at Richards Bay.

BELOW: Resident dolphins can be seen at all times of the year along the KZN coastline.

BELOW RIGHT: The SS Nebo, a British steamer that sank in 1884, was the first of many vessels to be wrecked at Aliwal Shoal, which makes for interesting diving.

BEACH AND SEA

It is thought that the upwelling water circulates southwards and combines with local riverine inputs, rather than joining the water north of Cape Vidal. This means that the seawater in the southern reaches may remain more nutrient-rich than that of Maputaland, and it could provide an explanation for the differences between the two regions.

Research of KZN's coastline and its biodiversity is undertaken primarily by the **Oceanographic Research Institute**, based at uShaka in Durban, and **Ezemvelo KZN Wildlife**. Further, more specialised research is carried out by various academic institutions and organisations such as **KZN Sharks Board**.

The Sardine Run

Sometime in June or July, the waters off the KZN coast appear quite chaotic as huge shoals of sardines move northwards during the spectacular Sardine Run. Followed by game fish and other predators, these amazing fish move from the southern Cape waters, forming enormous shoals along the way. Often the shoals are beached in nets by ski-boats or end up in the surf zone and people go crazy as in a carnival-like manner they wade into the water using buckets, bags or even just their T-shirts to catch 'sards'.

Sharks

Diving with sharks has become increasingly popular worldwide as people have learnt more about their importance and behaviour. In the summer months, shoals of game fish migrate to the warm KZN waters followed by sharks and game fish, but it is late winter that sees the arrival of one of the most popular sharks, the ragged-tooth sharks affectionately known as 'raggies'. After mating, the adults migrate northwards and from December to February, their gestation period, they can be seen off the Marine Reserve Section of iSimangaliso Wetland Park, adjacent to Sodwana Bay.

The **KZN Sharks Board**, based at uMhlanga, is one of the foremost shark research institutes in the world. Shark Board staff maintain the offshore nets

BELOW LEFT: *The annual Sardine Run, which causes great excitement among fishermen, visitors and locals, is one of the world's great migrations.*

BELOW: *Potato bass are the gentle giants of the ocean, often seen off the reefs of Sodwana Bay, Aliwal Shoal and other well-known dive spots.*

BEACH AND SEA

at the province's swimming beaches and they can be seen checking the nets by boat off the backline at sunrise. If the sharks caught in the nets are alive they are released. If they aren't, the boats take them back to the institute for research. As an alternative to the traditional nets, drumlines are now being used, which consists of a large, anchored float from which a single baited hook is suspended.

The KZN Sharks Board offers two ways to experience these creatures. Visitors can go to sea with their staff, to watch them check nets and learn about their work and sharks in general, or watch a fascinating and informative audiovisual followed by a shark dissection in the outdoor amphitheatre at their premises. Otherwise it is possible to dive with sharks at Aliwal Shoal, Sodwana Bay and Protea Banks, or at **uShaka Marine World** in Durban (see Playing Games p. 56).

Reefs and diving

The reefs of KZN provide outstanding diving opportunities. **Sodwana Bay** is regarded as one of the top 10 dive sites in the world. **Coral Divers**, a company of professional dive operators who run dive courses and offer dive charters from Sodwana Bay, can help divers get to the reefs, most of which are named according to their distance from the Jesse Point launch site. The variety of sharks,

BELOW: *Turtle tours to see giant leatherbacks take place from many of the lodges and camps in Maputaland.*

The Maputaland Sea Turtle Monitoring and Protection Programme

Started in 1963, the Sea Turtle Monitoring and Protection Programme in Maputaland is the longest continuously running research and protection project on leatherback and loggerhead turtles in the world. Since these creatures have been under protection, their growth has increased dramatically. Per season, approximately 250–350 leatherback and 2 500–3 000 loggerhead nests are recorded. While the leatherback figures are still significantly less than those of their loggerhead cousins, in the early 1960s the virtually total harvest of eggs by humans meant that the record low of nesting females was five.

Loggerheads found off the Maputaland coast have been known to swim distances of 2–3 000 kilometres to Madagascar, Zanzibar and other Indian Ocean islands. Leatherbacks are also great wanderers, swimming thousands of miles. One female that nested in Zululand was later recorded en route to Australia, having journeyed 7 000 kilometres in 5 months.

Leatherbacks have been around for about 65 million years and are possibly one of the largest reptiles left on Earth. There are only 28 known leatherback nesting sites around the world, and Maputaland is one of them.

extensive beds of staghorn, plate and mushroom corals, and various little coral creatures make for fascinating dives (see Playing Games p. 56).

The **Aliwal Shoal Marine Protected Area** includes a shallow reef system, which together with its warm water, high density and quantity of fish species – and most importantly, the opportunities it provides to dive with ragged-tooth and tiger sharks – attracts approximately 40 000 divers per year.

The reef itself is approximately 3 kilometres long and 300 metres wide, with a depth varying from 4 metres on the northeast pinnacle to 28 metres on its outer edges. It is located about 5 kilometres off the coast, slightly south of the Mkomazi River mouth. The shallowest and most popular section of the reef, the Crown, is some 380 metres wide and has an average depth of 12,5 metres.

Whales

Whaling was banned in 1975 and it took years for the populations to recover. The international ban on humpback whale hunting resulted in the population increasing by 10% annually.

Lately, there has been a greater variety and quantity of whales spotted off the KZN coastline, and there are some outstanding whale-watching opportunities, both from the shore and from charter boats.

Southern right and even orca have been spotted with increasing regularity. The beautiful, slow-swimming humpbacks are widely distributed and each year travel long distances, spending the summer months feeding on rich sources of krill in Antarctica before migrating northwards, arriving off the KZN coast in May or June. They breed off Mozambique's coast during winter months before starting their long migration back south during September and October.

Sea turtles

Although there are five sea turtle species found off KZN's coast (leatherback, loggerhead, green, hawksbill and olive ridley), only leatherback and loggerhead turtles nest in the area. Both species nest at night during the summer months, from October to March.

In a mystical, ancient ritual, the females move up the beach to well above the high-water mark, dig egg cavities with their flippers, lay their eggs and fill the hole in again, packing the sand down hard before returning to the sea.

Both turtle species' eggs take about 53–6 days to hatch. When ready to emerge, the little hatchlings cut their way out of the egg with a special egg tooth on the end of their beaks, dig their way out of their nest and scuttle towards the sea.

ABOVE: *Whales can be seen from permitted whale-watching charter boats near Shelley Beach and at other spots along the coast.*

8

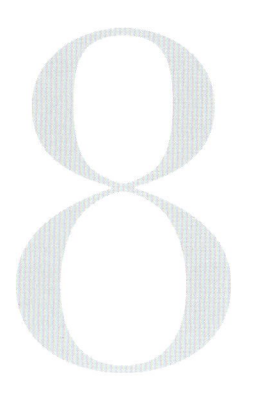

GAME AND NATURE PARKS

The first formally protected areas in Africa were KZN's Hluhluwe, Umfolozi and St Lucia game reserves, established in 1895. From these promising beginnings, a protected area network covering some 8% of the province, roughly 736 480 hectares, has been developed.

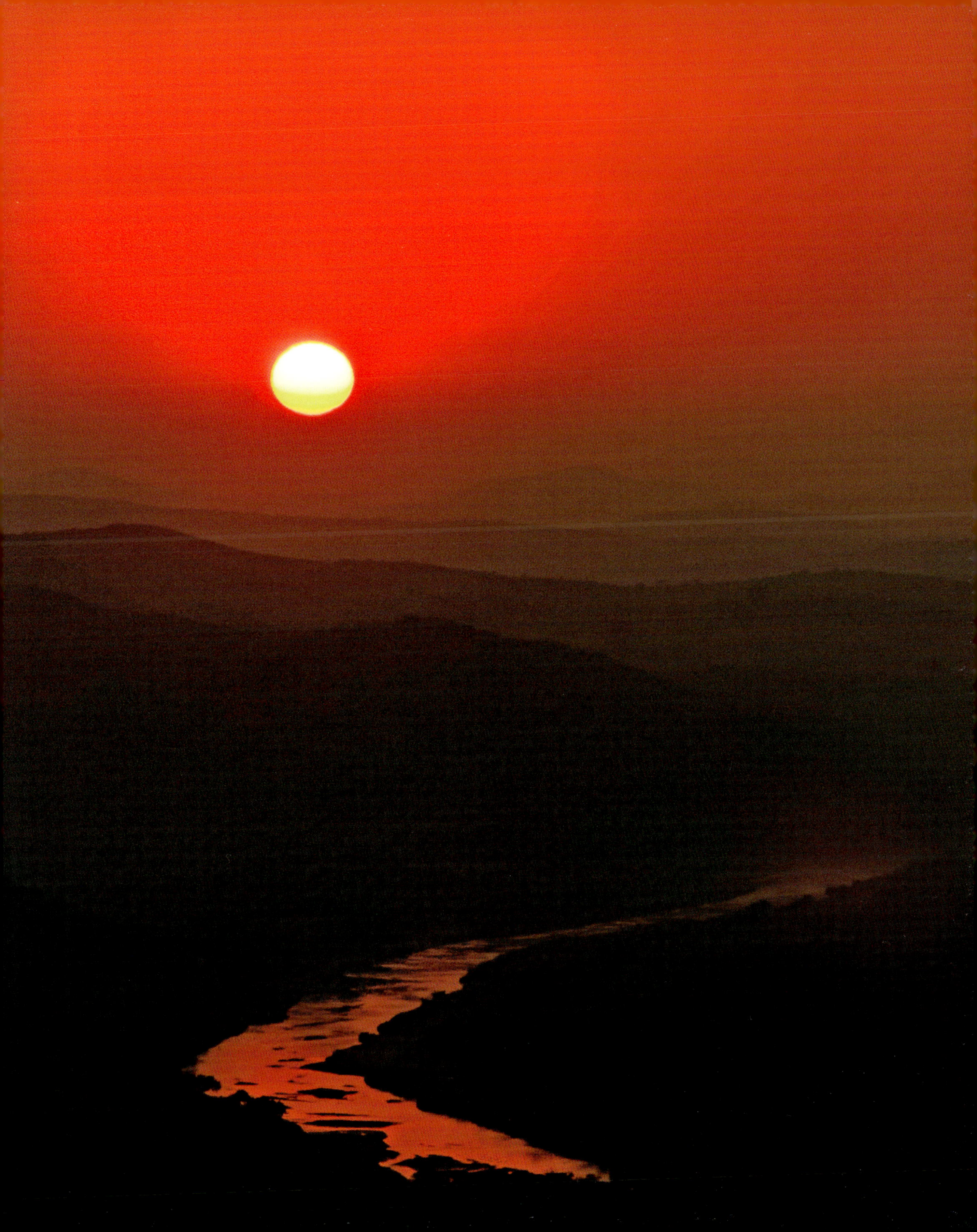

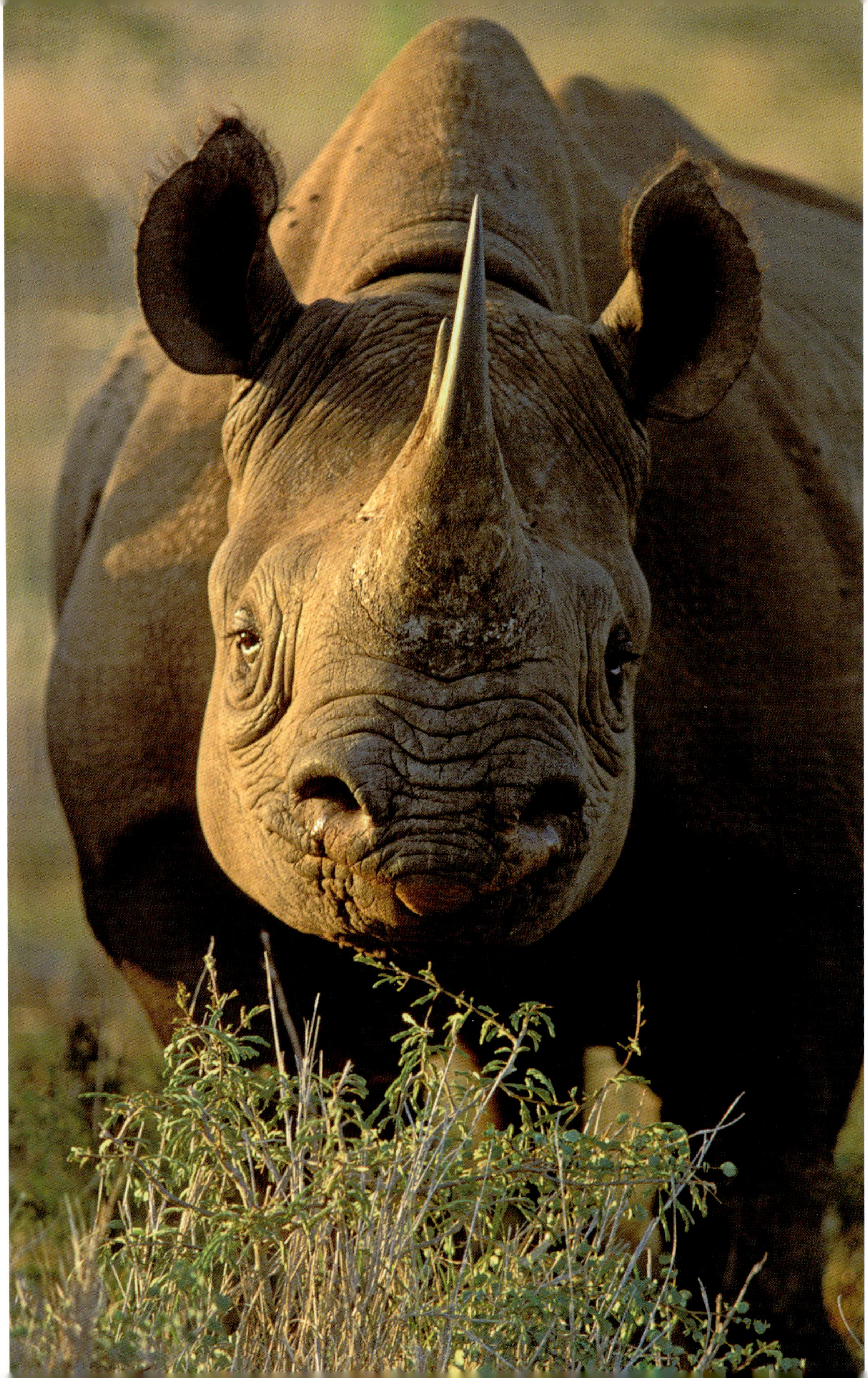

GAME AND NATURE PARKS

MANAGING THE WILDS

Ezemvelo KZN Wildlife, a parastatal body, administers more than 100 protected areas throughout KZN, including the uKhahlamba-Drakensberg Park World Heritage Site, and is the province's premier conservation organisation. The **iSimangaliso Wetland Park Authority** was established to develop and manage the iSimangaliso Wetland Park World Heritage Site.

The **Wildlife and Environment Society of South Africa** (WESSA) is an organisation that aims to contribute to the conservation of the planet's vitality and diversity. It is supported by some 2 400 members in KZN and 7 000 nationwide.

WESSA's role includes influencing policy- and decision-making, promoting sound environmental values and sustainable lifestyles and serving as an environmental watchdog, but perhaps its greatest contribution is through its vibrant and innovative environmental educational programme. The agenda benefits conservation and biodiversity education, not just provincially, but nationally and throughout the continent.

In KZN, much of WESSA's educational work takes place at **Umgeni Valley Nature Reserve** outside Howick. Attractions here include accommodation, walking trails, birds, wild animals, waterfalls, rock pools, cliffs, forests and grasslands as well as a river and an education centre. **Umbogavango**, on the South Coast near uMbogintwini, is a 36-hectare nature reserve that has 6 scenic trails, 5 bird hides and plenty of small mammals.

Another WESSA-owned and administered site is Durban's **Treasure Beach**, where the seashore and rocks can be explored by torchlight as part of the Rocky Shores Night Walks. Courses are continually run at **Twinstreams Education Centre** in the coastal forest of Mtunzini on the North Coast.

Msinsi Holdings manage areas surrounding the Shongweni, Nagle, Inanda, Albert Falls and Hazelmere Dam in a semi-private capacity. There are numerous other privately run protected areas that are governed by national and provincial conservation laws.

CONSERVATION EFFORTS
Operation Rhino

The recovery of the white rhinoceros from near extinction is one of the great success stories of African wildlife conservation. Operation Rhino was launched in 1960 when poaching and hunting had all but decimated Africa's entire rhinoceros population. The aim of the project was to transport surplus numbers of white rhinoceros from its base at Hluhluwe-iMfolozi Park – one of the few places that still had a barely viable population – to other protected areas.

By the end of 1996, the numbers of rhinoceros relocated worldwide had reached a total of more than 8 000, while approximately 7 000 had been resettled within South Africa.

Black Rhino Range Expansion Project

Operation Rhino has received enormous media attention for its success since its inception in the 1960s. However, the black rhinoceros has also been

PREVIOUS PAGE: *The sun rises over the Black Mfolozi River in the Hluhluwe-iMfolozi Park.*

OPPOSITE: *Hluhluwe-iMfolozi Park has gained international fame for re-establishing and protecting populations of rare black rhinoceros.*

ABOVE: *White rhinoceros, once almost extinct, are now plentiful in the Hluhluwe-iMfolozi Park.*

perilously close to extinction. During the 1970s and 1980s, poaching wiped out 96% of Africa's entire black rhinoceros population, leaving less than 3 000 animals in the wild.

In conjunctions with **Ezemvelo KZN Wildlife**, the **World Wide Fund For Nature South Africa** (WWF–SA) initiated the **Black Rhino Range Expansion Project** to protect and conserve these amazing, prehistoric-looking animals. Their aim is to increase the land available for black rhinoceros conservation, and thus alleviating the pressure on existing reserves. Populations have since been established in the Kruger National Park and Madikwe and Pilanesberg game reserves, among other locations. Further sites have been identified or are under consideration.

Zululand Rhino Reserve

Several landowners decided to combine their resources in a bid to protect endangered species, in particular black rhinoceros, in 2004. As such, they dropped their fences to establish the now 22 000-hectare **Zululand Rhino Reserve** as a rhinoceros release site. The following year, 21 black rhinoceros were introduced under the umbrella of the Black Rhino Range Expansion Project.

The extended reserve is not just a haven for these beasts, but for many other wild game species. The scenery is spectacular and there are a number of lodges to stay at, including **Leopard Mountain Game Lodge**, **Rhino River Lodge** and **Bayete Zulu Game Lodge**.

Rhino River Lodge offers welcoming and friendly staff, day and night drives, walking trails, an option of tracking rhinoceros and cheetah, and wonderful birding opportunities. Accommodation is in family lodges or reasonably priced luxury en suite rooms, and there is a swimming pool.

EZEMVELO KZN WILDLIFE'S MAJOR RESERVES
Hluhluwe-iMfolozi Park

In the 1920s, Hluhluwe-iMfolozi Park, close to uLundi, was the only remaining sanctuary of the southern white rhinoceros in the world, and it is from this reserve that most current populations emanate. It currently holds a little under a fifth of the global population, which has risen to some 10 000 – a massive leap from the 20-odd in 1900. There is also a substantial figure of black rhinoceros present.

Apart from rhinoceros, the park is also home to the other four members of the Big 5, namely elephant, lion, buffalo and leopard, as well as the rare endangered wild dog and a wide variety of other animals. Birdlife is also prolific, and there are more than 300 species.

There are a number of excellent lodges and bush camps in close vicinity to the park. Within its boundaries can be found the Hilltop and Mpila camps, both administered by Ezemvelo KZN Wildlife. **Hilltop Camp** has a luxury lodge and self-catering units, an à la carte restaurant, bar lounge, and gift and convenience shops. **Mpila Camp** is more basic, but has magnificent views of the wilderness area. Accommodation options include cottages, rest huts, safari tents and chalets.

Visitors can self-drive, take an open 4x4 game drive, enjoy a cruise on the Hluhluwe Dam or go for walks. There are several beautiful picnic sites, with ablution and braai facilities. The park runs some of the best wilderness trails in the country.

Wilderness trails

Going on a wilderness trail means experiencing nature, solitude and freedom from a human-controlled world, and enjoying a time of contemplation, quiet and timelessness in a way that is seldom possible these days. The opportunity to see big game while on foot, as opposed to from a vehicle, is also a thrilling experience.

The **iMfolozi Wilderness Trails** offer some of the best wilderness experiences in the province. They are set in the iMfolozi Wilderness Area, which covers 30 000 hectares in the Hluhluwe-iMfolozi Park. There are no roads, and human traffic is only permitted on foot, horseback or by canoe.

There are five trails here, catering to different preferences. The four-day **Base Camp Trail** takes trailists on a series of walks from a tented base camp, while the five-day **Primitive Trail** allows outdoors enthusiasts to combine a wilderness experience with backpacking and sleeping under the stars. Shorter versions of the trails, with some differences, are available.

ABOVE: *In places such as the iMfolozi Wilderness Area, wilderness trails provide visitors with wonderful opportunities to engage with nature, and see wild animals, on foot.*

GAME AND NATURE PARKS

Ithala Game Reserve

This 29 653-hectare game reserve, northeast of Vryheid, is perhaps one of KZN's most underrated conservation areas, yet scenically and from a game-viewing perspective it is outstanding, with great seasonal contrasts. It consists predominantly of rugged mountainous thornveld and open grassland areas, and overlooks Swaziland and the Pongola Valley. Although it has rhinoceros, elephant, buffalo and other big game, it does not carry lion, which leads to a more relaxed air among the plains animals and therefore sometimes offers more accessible viewing.

The reserve is interesting geologically – some rocks here dating back as much as three million years. **Ntshondwe**, the main camp, sits up against the Ntshondwe Cliffs, and has thatched chalets in among the wild figs, acacias and cabbage trees. The conference centre is often used as a wedding venue.

Ndumo Game Reserve

The reserve, which borders Mozambique, is at the southern limit for many tropical East African birds, and is famous for its birding. Also of note are the seasonal Banzi and Nyamiti pans, surrounded by giant sycamore figs and fever trees. For accommodation, there is a small camp site and 'squaredavels', and there is a little curio shop. Self-drive game viewing is possible, or visitors may go on a 4x4 tour or watch from a boat as crocodiles catch fish at the base of a small waterfall.

Tembe Elephant Park

Until 1983, the famous Tembe elephants made up the last free-ranging herd in South Africa, moving seasonally between Mozambique and Maputaland. During Mozambique's civil war the border fences were closed, ostensibly to protect the elephant. Under the recent Usuthu–Tembe–Futi Transfrontier Conservation Area agreement, the Tembe elephant will be able to roam freely again (see World Heritage Wetland p. 105).

Some 220-odd of these beasts, physically the largest elephants in South Africa, are currently protected within the reserve. As such, Tembe houses the province's largest indigenous elephant herd. Also to be seen from some of the strategically placed hides are the other Big 5 members.

There is only one tented camp in the sand forest and a limited number of cars is permitted entry per day, so it is best to plan ahead and arrive early.

Weenen Game Reserve

Based in the Midlands, this is a popular and pretty reserve for birding, camping and picnics. Game is also easily spotted in the African savannah here and at sites overlooking the Bushmans River Valley. Alternatively, white rhinoceros, giraffe and antelope may be watched from any of the several wonderful water holes.

PRIVATE GAME RESERVES

There are a number of outstanding private game reserves throughout KZN. Since the establishment

OPPOSITE: *One of the most loved and awe-inspiring members of the Big 5 is the elephant, found in many of KZN's protected areas.*

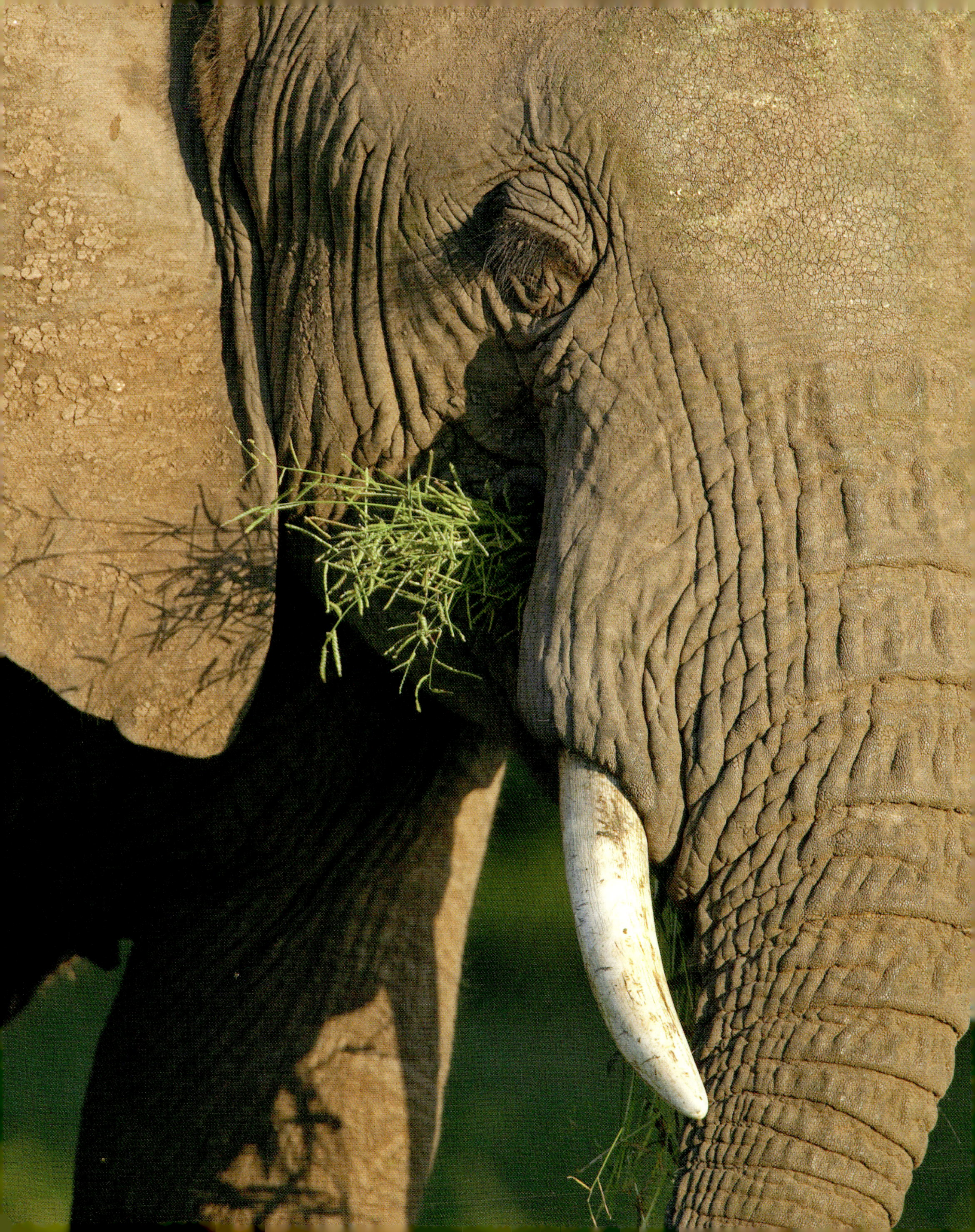

ABOVE: *The clear, fresh water in Ndumo Game Reserve's beautiful pans, such as Nyamithi Pan, draw animals, while the surrounding fever trees are attractive to birds.*

of **iSimangaliso Wetland Park** an increasing amount of private game lodges have been developed in the surrounding area.

Phinda Private Game Reserve, one of the first private reserves, is in the centre of a vast, ecologically diverse region. This Big 5 luxury reserve offers everything a discerning traveller could want, from outstanding day and night game drives to river boat trips, turtle and whale watching and a flight in a small aircraft. There are very different lodges in each ecological region of the reserve.

It is hard to imagine a more opulent bush lodge than **Thanda Private Game Reserve** – replete with health spa. The accommodation is in amazing villas with cosy fireplaces, private heated splash pools, private bomas for intimate dining and open-air salas high over the reserve, with stunning views. Guests will be hard-pressed to leave the lap of luxury to go on a game drive.

NATURE RESERVES AND CONSERVANCIES

Sport fishing is one of the primary attractions of **Phongolo Nature Reserve**, situated close to Swaziland's southernmost border. The Pongola River and Pongolapoort Dam are the southernmost range for tigerfish, making the latter the site for the annual September Tigerfish Bonanza. It can get exceedingly hot in summer, but the 300 species of birds and excellent game viewing still make it a worthwhile option.

South of Richards Bay on the North Coast, **Enseleni Nature Reserve** has some great walks through the coastal grasslands and forest, while the Nseleni River provides a freshwater habitat that draws some good birds. It is a botanical paradise.

Moving south, about 2 kilometres from Mtunzini, the small, 1 000-odd-hectare **uMlalazi Nature Reserve** includes a pleasant coastal dune forest and swampland, numerous small mammals, such as bushbuck, duiker and reedbuck, and a surprising variety of birds. Hiking, fishing and swimming are available, as is limited water-skiing in the lagoon – watch out though, as crocodiles and sharks might be present.

The tiny **Harold Johnson Nature Reserve** is located on the south bank of the uThukela River, about 100 kilometres north of Durban. It protects many small mammals and birds, fascinating plants and 114 species of butterfly. Two historic Anglo–Zulu War heritage sites, namely Fort Pearson and the Ultimatum Tree, are found within the reserve.

Inland in Zululand, in eShowe, the small indigenous forest reserves of **Entumeni** and **Dlinza** have become more popular since the establishment of the 125-metre-long **Dlinza Forest Aerial Boardwalk**, owned by the local community. It allows visitors to walk through the forest canopy, stopping at the 20-metre-high viewing tower overlooking giant umzimbeet, yellowwoods and other special trees. It is a treat for nature lovers, boasting some 440 bird species, butterflies, insects and small mammals.

Closer to Durban, near the popular resort village of uMhlanga Rocks, beachgoers can take a short trail through the **uMhlanga Lagoon Nature Reserve**, which protects the estuary, dune and coastal forests, to access the beach.

Beachwood Mangrove Nature Reserve, on the banks of the Mgeni River, Durban, is a heritage site protecting the mangrove swamp forest and estuary. **Kenneth Stainbank Nature Reserve** in Durban, with its habituated wild game, is popular with families for short hikes, braais and picnics. Also in Durban is **Giba Gorge**, popular with families and for mountain biking.

On the South Coast, **Vernon Crookes Nature Reserve** protects coastal scarp forest and coastal

Malaria

Malaria has been substantially reduced in KZN in recent years, and in most cases poses no immediate threat to visitors (see World Heritage Wetland p. 105).

Travellers to the area are still advised to take precautions, even if the chance of infection is minimal. The female *Anopheles* mosquito, which carries the virus, feeds at night, so this is the time to be vigilant. Visitors should wear long-sleeved shirts, use mosquito sprays and sleep under mosquito nets. There are also several excellent antimalarial medications on the market, and any travel clinic or doctor will be able to advise travellers accordingly.

Symptoms of infection are often similar to that of influenza, but can include headache, nausea, fever and vomiting. Malaria is easily treatable and symptoms should not be ignored. If any of these conditions are experienced a doctor should be consulted immediately.

GAME AND NATURE PARKS

grasslands. Scenic walks allow visitors to see many small mammals and birds. The elusive tree hyrax, or tree dassie, while not easily seen, may be heard.

Children will love **Dlangala Wildlife Sanctuary**, where injured wild animals are nurtured back to health and released into the wild. It is located in the uMkomaas Valley, which is a true bushveld environment with excellent birding, game drives (including night drives), fishing, hiking, 4x4 trails, horse-riding and tubing down the river. Stay overnight at one of the little bush or river camps or in the thatched self-catering bungalow.

uVongo's **Skyline Nature Reserve** has an arboretum that includes some 76 indigenous coastal tree species. It is ideal for walks and picnics when the weather for the beach is unsuitable.

Oribi Gorge Nature Reserve, located in one of KZN's most dramatic settings, has steep cliffs, forests, gorges and rivers, and is a great place for adventure activities (see Playing Games pp. 57–8).

Mpenjati Nature Reserve, south of Margate, is popular for fishing, boating, canoeing and swimming. It has two picnic spots, which have braai facilities and ablution blocks.

KZN's southernmost reserve is **Umtamvuna Nature Reserve**, which protects a pretty stretch of riverine forest and steep rocky cliffs. In spring, it hosts stunning displays of spring wild flowers.

BELOW: *The Mtamvuna River Gorge, near Port Edward on the South Coast, has a lovely nature reserve.*

Located inland in the Midlands, the **Karkloof Conservation and Tourism Centre** near Howick is a great place to spend a few hours in either the Gartmore or Loskop bird hides. Blue, grey crowned and wattled cranes, herons, African fish-eagles and various water birds are residents and the dams are stocked with bass and blue gill.

Boating and fishing are the main activities at **Wagendrift Dam and Nature Reserve** near Estcourt. An Iron Age site, dating back to about CE 1300 and listed as the first Iron Age settlement in Southern Africa, is located within the reserve.

Smaller mountain reserves include **Mount Currie** near Kokstad, **Himeville** near Underberg and **Highmoor**, north of Kamberg. Mount Currie's Adam Kok Laager Site and the Boy Scout add a historical feel to the old cattle-track hiking paths. Himeville has a captive breeding site for all three crane species and offers access to Lesotho in 4x4s, and Highmoor has two well-stocked trout dams and two caves, Caracal and Aasvoël, where hikers can overnight.

TAMING THE WILDS
Gardens

South Africa has nine national botanical gardens, administered by the **South African National Biodiversity Institute** (SANBI), which showcase South Africa's unique and diverse floral wealth.

Pietermaritzburg's elegant 49-hectare **KZN National Botanical Garden** is divided into two sections: indigenous and exotic. It specialises in the conservation of plants from the eastern region of the country but also includes rare and endangered species from elsewhere.

Pietermaritzburg experiences marked seasonal changes, which means the gardens, too, are constantly changing. The restaurant under the trees is close to a lily-filled duck pond where children can feed the water birds. Regular music concerts are held and guided walks can be arranged.

This oasis of green that is **Durban Botanic Gardens** provides a lush break from the frenzy of the city. The big leafy fig trees and other plants

ABOVE: *The thatched-roofed Mpila Camp, in the iMfolozi section of Hluhluwe-iMfolozi Park, provides just one of many excellent accommodation options for visitors to the area.*

ABOVE: *The KZN National Botanical Garden in Pietermaritzburg, established in the early 1870s, provides a quiet, green retreat from the bustle of city life.*

OPPOSITE: *The Dlinza Forest Aerial Boardwalk, near eShowe, is a beautiful place to learn more about the trees and birds of KZN.*

collected from around the world surround a central pond where hundreds of birds come to roost. There are sensory and herb gardens, giant cycads and lovely lawns, and there is an orchid house. Guided walks are on offer and a full programme of music concerts take place in the gardens.

The privately owned **Makaranga Garden Lodge** has the most magnificent garden. Paths wend their way under the huge makaranga trees, around the string of leafy lakes and waterfalls, over little stone bridges, past tinkling streams, beautiful green undergrowth, vines, ferns, clivias and stunning garden sculptures, and out onto the lawns and fabulous indigenous koppies. Tea is served on the verandah.

One of the largest private collections of Shona statues can be viewed in the gardens, and there is a stunning collection of African artwork in and around the lodge and conference centre.

Barn Swallows

From November to April, an estimated 3 million barn swallows make their way to the **Mount Moreland Wetlands** in the Lake Victoria Conservancy, near uMdloti on the North Coast, for winter roosting – some 13% of the world's total. Some of the swallows are only 3 months old when they leave the UK, Denmark and Scandinavia to make this incredible 6 000-kilometre journey down the east coast of Africa. It is not known why the swallows return to the same site every year, but it is likely that their behaviour is genetically determined.

A viewing site has been established for the public. The ideal time to see the swallows is at sunset, and visitors should bring their own chairs, refreshments and insect repellent.

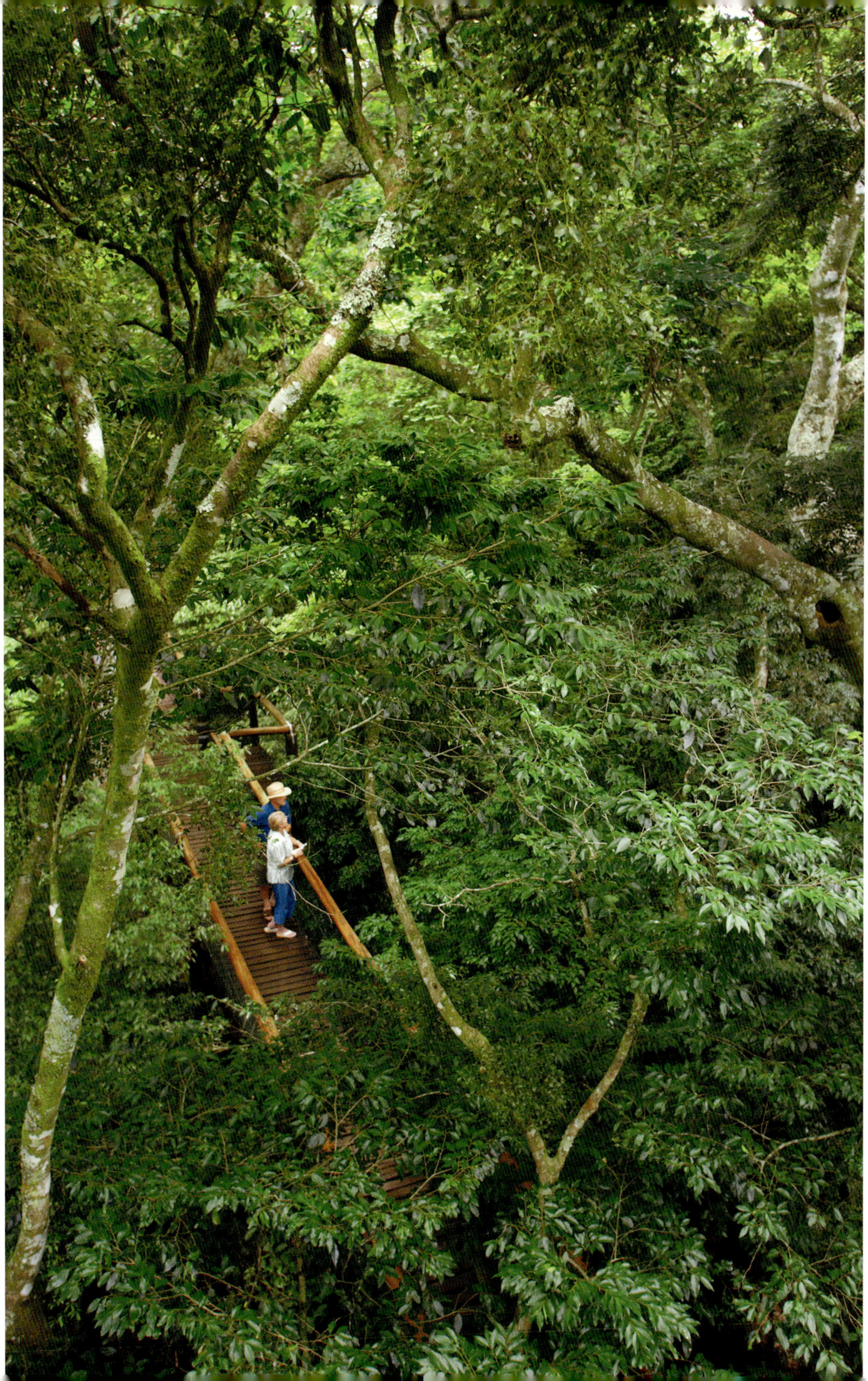

9

WORLD HERITAGE WETLAND

Nelson Mandela said it best: '[iSimangaliso] must be the only place on the globe where the world's oldest land mammal (the rhinoceros) and the world's biggest terrestrial mammal (the elephant) share an ecosystem with the world's oldest fish (the coelacanth) and the world's biggest marine mammal (the whale).'

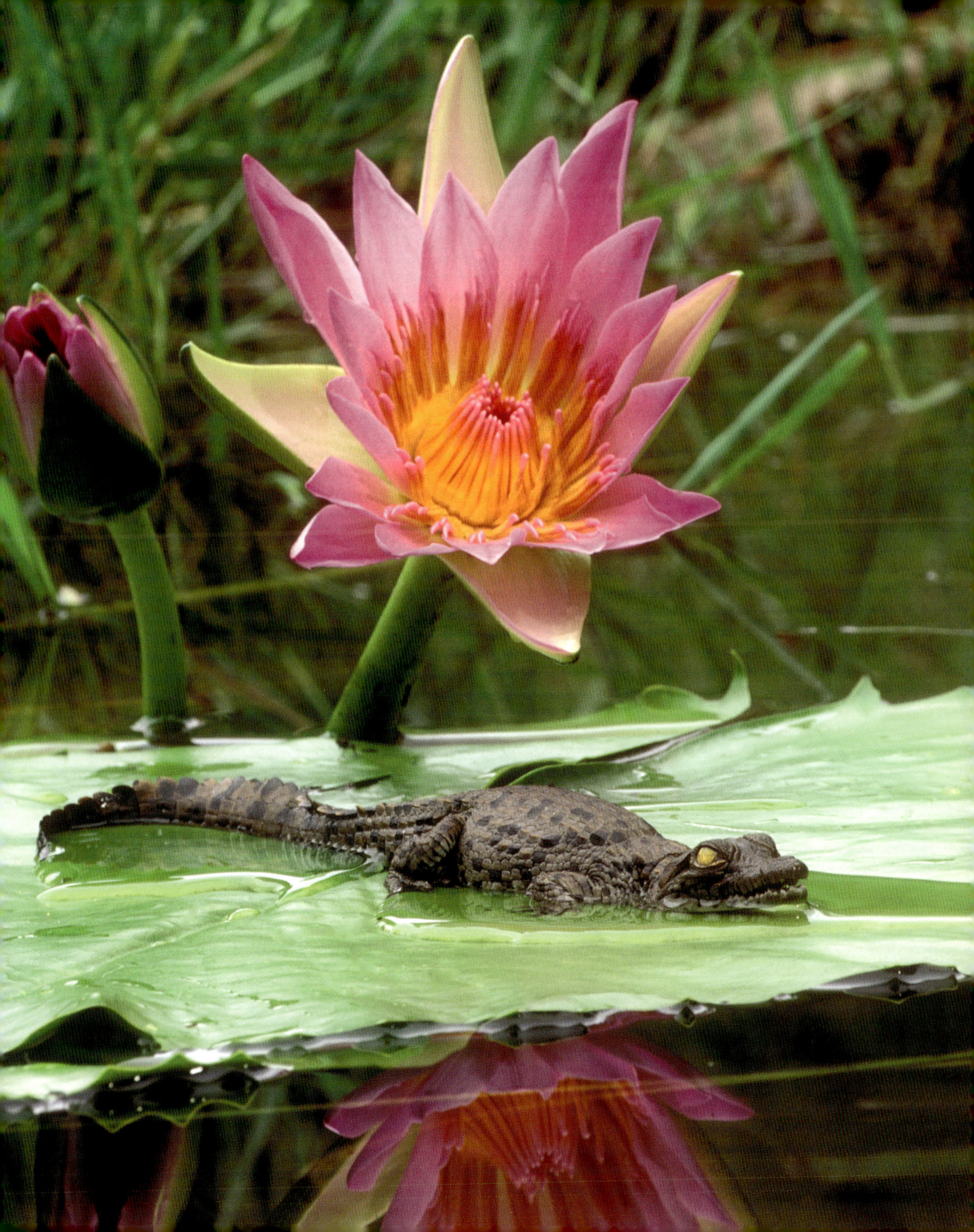

WORLD HERITAGE WETLAND

ISIMANGALISO WETLAND PARK

In December 1999 **iSimangaliso Wetland Park** (IWP) was proclaimed a World Heritage Site – South Africa's first. While it may hold enormous significance for world conservation, it holds an even greater place in the hearts of ordinary South Africans, masses of whom took part in one of the greatest conservation campaigns ever seen in the country. In 1990, along with Nelson Mandela and Mangosuthu Buthelezi, millions of concerned citizens signed a petition to save the then Greater St Lucia Wetlands Park from being mined.

iSimangaliso means 'something miraculous' in Zulu. The park covers about a third of the entire KZN coast and is surrounded by several major game reserves in the broader Maputaland region. The spin-offs for visitors are enormous. It is possible to spend the morning on the beach and the afternoon in a game reserve. Within a couple of hours, visitors can fish, bird-watch, see turtles hatching and witness a lion kill in a neighbouring reserve.

Lake St Lucia, which forms a central part of the IWP, supports populations of crocodile and hippo as well as rhinoceros, buffalo, waterbuck, impala, nyala, kudu and a host of other wild animals. The amazing diversity of habitats within and around the park, from the Lebombo Mountains to grasslands and forests, wetlands, mangroves and vegetated dunes, all contribute to the diversity of animal life.

IWP protects 10 unique areas. Stretching from Maphelane in the south to Kosi Bay in the north, it incorporates Lake St Lucia/St Lucia Estuary, Cape Vidal and the Eastern Shores, Charters Creek and the Western Shores, False Bay, Sodwana Bay, uMkhuze, Lake Sibaya and Coastal Forest. Four sections of the park have been registered as Wetlands of International Importance.

The **iSimangaliso Wetland Park Authority** protects the park while making it an accessible and enjoyable tourist destination that can sustain livelihoods for the five cultural groups that live in the area, namely Zulu, Swazi, Shangaan, Tsonga and Gonda speakers.

As such, the region is developed in such a way that it benefits both nature and humans, and a level of cooperation between countries bordering the province and IWP is necessary as they are interlinked in so many ways.

Important biological features

iSimangaliso is 332 000 hectares in size and has 220 kilometres of coastline. Consisting of five ecosystems (eight including the surrounding areas), it is the largest estuarine system in Africa. The lake system is made up of two estuarine-linked lakes, St Lucia and Kosi, and four large freshwater lakes with several bird-rich islands.

The location on the coast between subtropical and tropical Africa has resulted in an exceptional biodiversity. The park protects 526 species of birds, giving it the greatest avifauna diversity in Africa.

Not only does it have the highest number and density of black rhinoceros anywhere in the world,

PREVIOUS PAGE: Nile crocodile hatchlings can commonly be seen among the lilies in iSimangaliso Wetland Park.

OPPOSITE: Interesting mangrove forests can be found along the Maputaland coast.

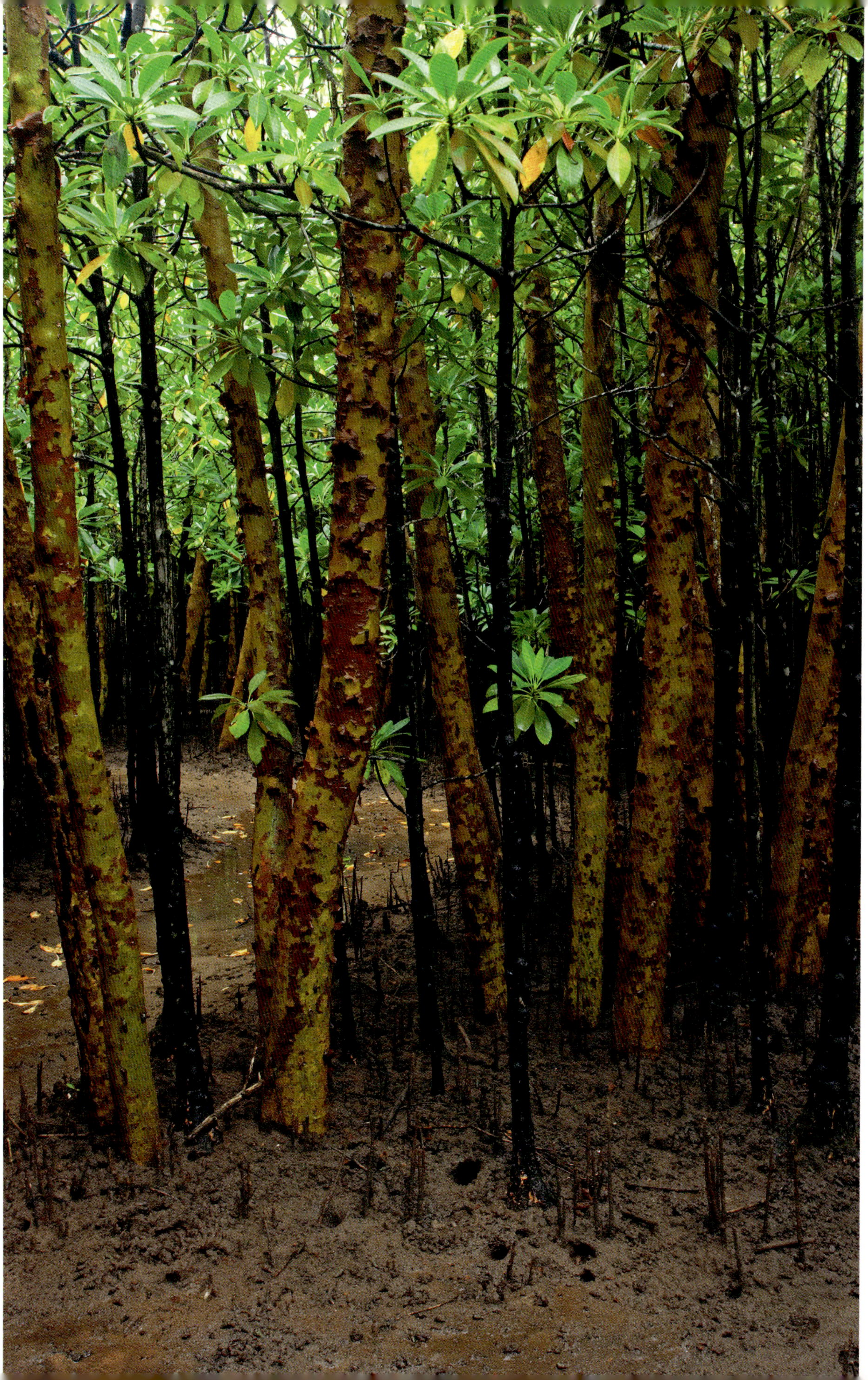

WORLD HERITAGE WETLAND

but there are 80 species of dragonfly, 110 species of butterfly and more than 2 000 species of flowering plants. All five of South Africa's surviving mangrove tree species exist in IWP.

There are also 36 snake species (including the rare and endangered Gaboon adder) and 35 frog species – the highest number in Southern Africa, 2 of which are endemic. Approximately 50 resident species are listed as threatened internationally, while about 150 and 105 are on the CITES and Red Data lists respectively.

The southernmost extension of coral reefs in Africa occurs here, as well as magnificent submarine canyons in which a population of coelacanths, once thought to be extinct, can be found. The marine life includes five species of sea turtles, two of which are threatened nesting sea turtles, as well as whales, dolphins and whale sharks. An incredible variety of fish and 100 species of coral have been recorded.

The coastal dune system is estimated to be 25 000 years old, consisting of linear dunes of up to 180 metres in height – among the highest forested dunes in the world. The inland Western Shores exhibit ancient shoreline terraces, fossil marine life, sand forest and dry savannah vegetation.

TRANSFRONTIER CONSERVATION AREAS

The Ponto do Ouro–Kosi Bay Transfrontier Conservation Area (TFCA) is a bilateral marine and coastal arrangement between IWP and the Ponta do Ouro–Inhaca coastline of Mozambique. It is designed to greatly benefit biodiversity, wetland protection and sea turtle conservation, as the region contains breeding grounds of both leatherback and loggerhead turtles.

It is also part of the **Lubombo Transfrontier Conservation and Resource Area**. Along with

BELOW: *iSimangaliso Wetland Park was declared a World Heritage Site because, among other reasons, it protects rare and endangered species, such as the beautiful Gaboon adder.*

BELOW RIGHT: *A number of reptile species, including the pretty green tree frog, can be found in iSimangaliso.*

WORLD HERITAGE WETLAND

five Ramsar sites, the initiative encompasses five distinct TFCAs between Mozambique, South Africa and Swaziland.

The Lubombo Conservancy–Goba TFCA includes the Hlane Game Sanctuary, Mbuluzi Game Reserve, Nkhalashane Ranch and the Shewula Community Nature Reserve in Swaziland and Goba community land in Mozambique.

The Usuthu–Tembe–Futi TFCA incorporates conservation and resource use areas in South Africa, such as Tembe Elephant Park and Ndumo Game Reserve, with reserves in Mozambique and Swaziland, making it a trilateral TFCA. It has the potential of uniting an ancient elephant population that used to move freely between Mozambique and South Africa.

The Nsubane–Phongolo TFCA combines land surrounding South Africa's Phongolo Nature Reserve with protected areas in Swaziland.

Malaria programme in iSimangaliso

Malaria is a most notorious killer and is considered to be one of the biggest deterrents for tourism development. However, one of the big projects undertaken by the IWP authorities, together with many other government and non-government groups, has been to establish a serious cross-border push to reduce the high levels of malaria once experienced in the region.

The project has been enormously successful. Malaria in the South African section of the Lubombo was reduced by 98% while the Swaziland and Mozambique sections were reduced by 85% and 65% respectively. For the first time in history Lake St Lucia is malaria-free (see Game and Nature Parks p. 95).

BELOW LEFT: *While usually difficult to spot, the male southern tree agama makes it easier for visitors when he is in breeding, by taking on bright cobalt-blue colouring.*

BELOW: *Amphibious African mudhoppers can be seen on muddy banks and in mangrove swamps.*

WORLD HERITAGE WETLAND

The last TFCA in the Lubombo Transfrontier Conservation and Resource Area is also between South Africa and Swaziland. The Songimvelo–Malolotja TFCA links South Africa's Josefsdal Songimvelo Game Reserve with Swaziland's Malolotja Nature Reserve and protects the Drakensberg Escarpment and the highlands and mountains known as the Barberton Mountains.

HISTORY AND CONCERVATION
Fossils and archaeological sites

Along the western shores of Lake St Lucia are banks rich in marine fossils, which indicate that the area was once inhabited by long-extinct molluscs, delicate nautiluses and relatives of clams. Enormous 16-centimetre-long shark's teeth have also been found there. Both animal and coral fossils can be viewed at the interpretive centre.

Coelacanths

In 1938, a dead coelacanth was 'caught' by a fishing trawler near East London. As they were thought to have been extinct for 70 million years, the discovery captured the imagination of the world. These fish are living fossils dating back 450 million years and provide an extraordinary window into the past.

Following the discovery of a population off the Comoros Islands and the subsequent finds off the island of Sulawesi in Indonesia, scientists began

BELOW: In iSimangaliso, large herds of antelope, such as of the greater kudu, can be seen against a backdrop of some of the largest vegetated dunes in the world.

WORLD HERITAGE WETLAND

to realise that the species was considerably more widespread. In 2000, a group of divers amazed the world again when they encountered a population of coelacanths in IWP at a depth of just over 100 metres. It is very rare to find coelacanths in such shallow water, so accessible for research.

Elephant reintroductions

In August 2001, 20 elephants from the Hluhluwe-iMfolozi Park were released on the eastern shores of iSimangaliso. Later, a further 12 were brought in, followed by another 8 from the Kruger National Park. There are presently about 60 elephants roaming IWP as they once did, adding a majestic dimension to a visit there.

Rare, Threatened & Endemic Species Project

This project was initiated by **Ezemvelo KZN Wildlife**, **iSimangaliso Wetland Park Authority** and the **Wildlands Conservation Trust** in 2003 to update information on the presence and distribution of rare, threatened and/or endemic species, with a specific focus on groups such as reptiles, amphibians, smaller mammals, beetles, birds and orchids. Research has been conducted on animals such as the endangered Gaboon adder.

During a 2006 survey in uMkhuze, two species – the tiny musk shrew and the striped harlequin snake – were recorded for the first time. So were the pygmy wolf snake and Wahlberg's epauletted fruit

WORLD HERITAGE WETLAND

ABOVE: *Hippo can be seen and heard swimming about and grunting to each other in the many pretty pans and rivers in iSimangaliso.*

OPPOSITE: *Kosi Bay mouth, protected by the forested peninsula, is where iSimangaliso's beautiful string of lakes joins the sea.*

bat. Altogether some 150 species have been added to the World Heritage Schedules so far; extended distributions of 24 species have been recorded; and several sightings of about 90 rare, threatened and/or endemic species have been recorded.

CULTURAL TOURISM

The local people living around the park, many of whom depend on its natural resources for survival, have continued to play an integral part in the park. The iSimangaliso Wetland Park Authority has taken the alleviation of poverty and the promotion of development within the surrounding communities, two of its most important tasks, very seriously.

There have been a number of **job-creation initiatives**, such as the construction of roads and fences and the Land Care Programme, which encompasses the clearing of alien vegetation and land rehabilitation. The establishment of roads has benefited tourism, made clinics, health services and education facilities accessible to the rural poor and enabled poor traders to reach their markets.

New restaurants, B&Bs, shops and services have also been established in the area to cater to IWP tourists, which have helped provide employment for the locals. Also look out for craft markets, both on roadsides and at the entrances to reserves and camp sites.

A craft programme was established to train local crafters, assist in the development of products and link them to markets (see Creative Thinking p. 45). Other cultural projects encompass music, drama, dance and photography.

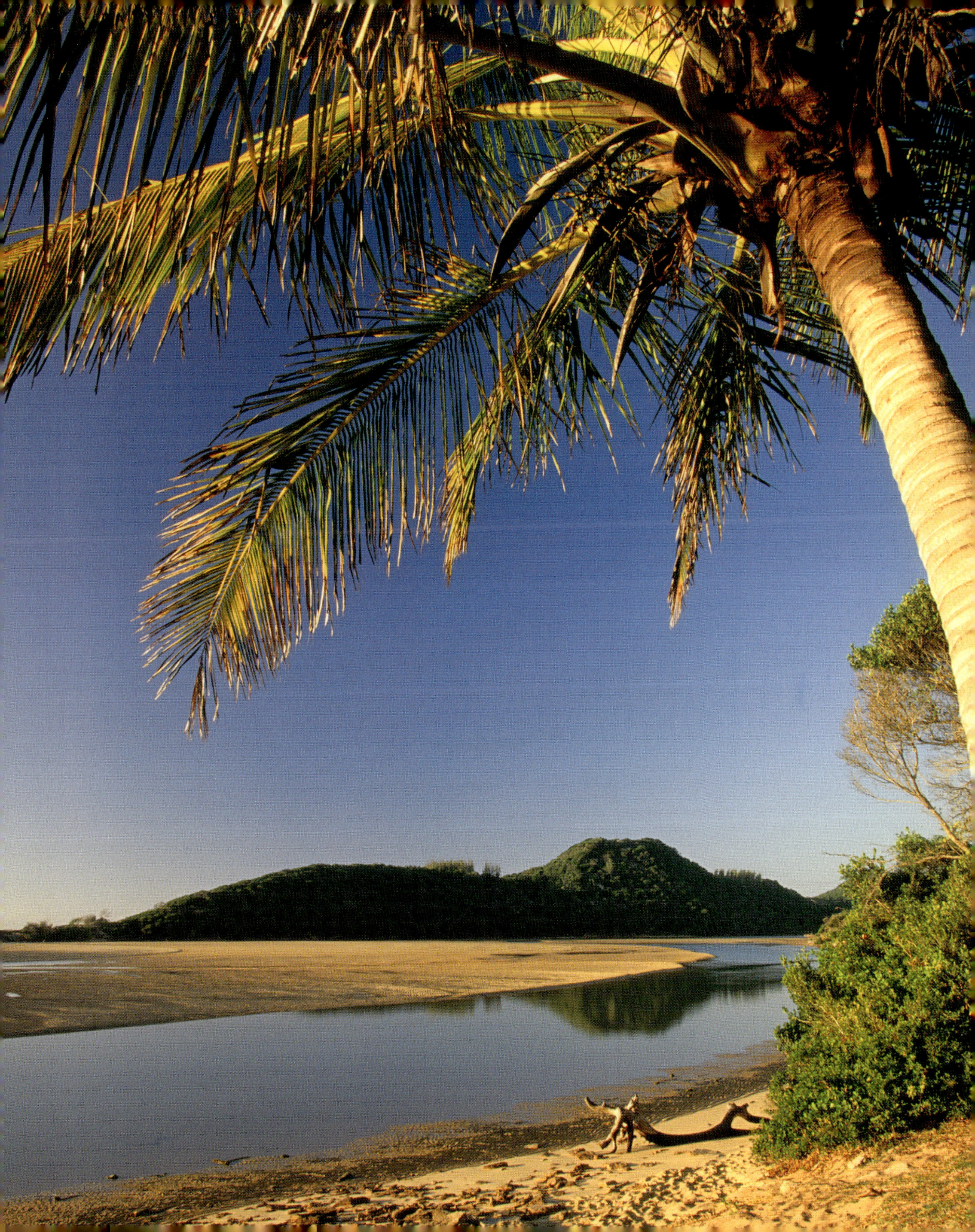

ABOVE: *Fishermen clear their ancient fish traps in Kosi Bay, in the far north of iSimangaliso Wetland Park.*

iNcema

As part of IWP's Community Based Natural Resource Harvesting Project, a section of *iNcema* reed beds is set aside annually for local women in the community to cut and collect. *iNcema* plays an economically significant and culturally important role in the lives of many rural people, and IWP is one of the few remaining sites where the reeds can still be harvested. Due to foresight and responsible planning, it has been conserved in the park and because of this, large quantities continue to grow. Many negotiations with local tribal authorities and user groups take place to ensure that the *iNcema* is harvested sustainably.

Approximately 3500 women arrive in April or May to begin the harvest, and the harvest festival usually lasts two to three weeks. IWP field rangers are on standby to ensure the harvesters are safe from the buffalo, hippo and elephant often found in and around the reed beds.

The traditional *fonya*

A number of water pans are found in this region – particularly up towards Kosi Bay. Some dry up completely during winter and only start to fill again in the rainy summer season. In the old days, usually when the water levels were getting low, local men, armed with spears, would get together, collect their distinctive *fonya* baskets and head for the pans.

A group would start at one end and in a long row, beat or chase the fish, isolating a shoal and using the baskets to trap them. The hole at the top of the *fonya* basket is where a person can grab or stab fish with a spear.

These days, many women are also involved in fish drives. It is a noisy, happy occasion. It is hard to pin down exactly when a *fonya* will take place, because as the locals say, 'it happens when the time is right'. Ask a resident or a staff member. If a *fonya* drive is about to take place, an invitation to go along may be extended.

Interestingly, *fonya* baskets have become popular with tourists who often convert them into ethno-chic lampshades.

Ancient fish traps

In Makhawulani, the first of Kosi Bay's four lakes, there are a number of fish traps, or fish kraals as they are sometimes known. These kraals, some of them dating back some 700 years, have been built and maintained by generations of Tsonga people, who are excellent and knowledgeable fishing folk. Each kraal is owned by an individual family and is handed down through the generations.

Almost sculptural in shape, the kraals are carefully positioned in the beautiful clear waters of the estuary, where passing fish swim in through a maze of thin-poled fences that have been woven through with reeds. The smaller fish can escape, but the larger fish are guided into the circular kraal and trapped there. The traps are checked at regular intervals throughout the day, and fish are speared or caught by hand. The traps can be seen from afar, but it is best to arrange a boat to get closer. Try to visit when the fishermen are clearing their traps.

PLACES TO STAY

There are a various accommodation options on offer, from lodges to camp sites. The majority of bookings can be made through **Ezemvelo KZN Wildlife**. Some of the camps have limited fresh water, and are sometimes closed due to a lack of this valuable resource. Visitors should check with Ezemvelo KZN Wildlife prior to going to see if their chosen camp is operational, especially False Bay Park, Fanie's Island, Charters Creek and Mabibi, which are the sites most affected.

There are two camps at **Cape Vidal** – one right on the beach, then a fishing camp situated on the small inland Lake Bhangazi, which is available for small groups. The log cabins, fishing cabins

ABOVE: *Tsonga fishermen still use an age-old method of trapping fish in a* fonya *basket.*

ABOVE: *The wooden chalets at Cape Vidal, popular with families and anglers, are situated just behind the beach's dunes.*

and camp site are all popular. The area has great ski-boat fishing and there is a good whale-watch tower where visitors can view these migrating beasts. Hiking is good and there are a number of self-guided trails through the coastal forest.

Maphelane has a camp site and chalets and is best known for its ski-boat fishing and surf angling. The rocky outcrops are good for mussel picking and crayfishing. Remember, permits are required.

On the inland shores of Lake St Lucia is **False Bay Park**, geologically one of the oldest areas, with its pleasant hikes, boating and game viewing. There are camp sites along the shore overlooking the lake, while Dungandlovu Rustic Camp has four huts, each equipped with four beds.

Further down the western shores of the lake is the secluded **Fanie's Island**, popular with anglers and bird-watchers. There is a fossil interpretive centre and self-guided walking trails are on offer, as well as hutted accommodation and camp sites.

uMkhuze has the Inhlonhlela and Insumo pans, home to large communities of hippo and crocodile. Some 400 bird species have been recorded here, and can be observed from one of six hides. Four two-bed sleeping units with en suite bathrooms are available, and meals are cooked by the staff.

Kosi Bay is actually not a bay, but an estuary comprising a chain of four freshwater lakes, alive with hippos, crocodiles and a diversity of fish, that stretches 18 kilometres before entering the sea. While there is fishing throughout, good salt-water fly-fishing can be done at the mouth, where snorkelling is also legendary.

The camp is situated on the western shore of Lake Nhlange, and while the road is quite sandy it can be accessed by sedan cars. To go anywhere further than the camp and explore the surrounds, however, will require the use of 4x4 vehicles.

Known internationally as a premier dive site, **Sodwana Bay** is also an excellent ski-boat fishing region with record catches of both sailfish and billfish. During season the beach is packed with scuba operators and wetsuit-clad bodies, but it is still possible to find a patch of beach to picnic on, and snorkelling in the rock pools is fun. There are 10 5-bed and 10 8-bed log cabins, which all have bathroom, kitchen and braai facilities. Alternatively there are extensive camping amenities on offer.

Lake Sibaya, at 77 square kilometres, is South Africa's largest freshwater lake. It is easily as beautiful and unspoiled as Kosi Bay – the water is so clear that underwater hippos and crocodiles can often be seen – but it has no outlet to the sea. Great coastal dune forests loom between the fresh water and the ocean. The rustic **Mabibi Coastal Camp**, for which a 4x4 is required, is a five-minute walk from the beach. It is a great spot for snorkelling, swimming, fishing and bird-watching.

Private options include the upmarket **Thonga Beach Lodge**, right in front of the dunes at Lake Sibaya, making it possible to walk directly onto the beach. It offers turtle drives, good snorkelling, diving and swimming.

Further down is Wilderness Safari's **Rocktail Beach Camp** where turtle monitoring and trips into the local community can be arranged. There is a good dive centre nearby and the brave can dive with pregnant ragged-tooth sharks.

THINGS TO DO

To really experience the Eastern Shores, take a hike along the **Mziki Trail**. This fantastic three-

ABOVE: *A highlight of any visit to a game reserve or park is a night in a tented camp, such as here at uMkhuze.*

WORLD HERITAGE WETLAND

BELOW: *A canoe trail through the channels around Kosi Bay gives visitors a chance to really experience life in one of the world's great wetlands.*

OPPOSITE: *The female African fish-eagle (left) is slightly larger than her male counterpart (right).*

day hike takes in all the ecosystems, including stretches of beaches inaccessible to day visitors. The IWP offers fantastic opportunities for **scuba diving** and **snorkelling**. From June to November, **watch whales** on their annual migration from their feeding grounds in the Antarctic to their breeding grounds off Mozambique and Madagascar.

The ancient **turtle breeding ritual** takes place between November and March. There are **deep-sea boat tours** as well as **boat trips** on St Lucia Lake to see some of the hippos and crocodiles. Learn more about the Nile crocodile at the **St Lucia Crocodile Centre**. **Horse safaris** are available on the beach and in the game park, even for those without much experience, and a **canoe trail** is an excellent way to do some bird-watching.

Also of interest are the red sand ridges, which are ancient dunes, and the astonishing diversity of habitats, from the Lebombo mountain range to broad stretches of acacia savannah, swamps, woodlands and riverine forests.

There is also an unusual sand forest found in the heart of the reserve at uMkhuze where the rare and diminutive suni antelope can be seen. **Guided walks** and day and night **game drives** can be arranged.

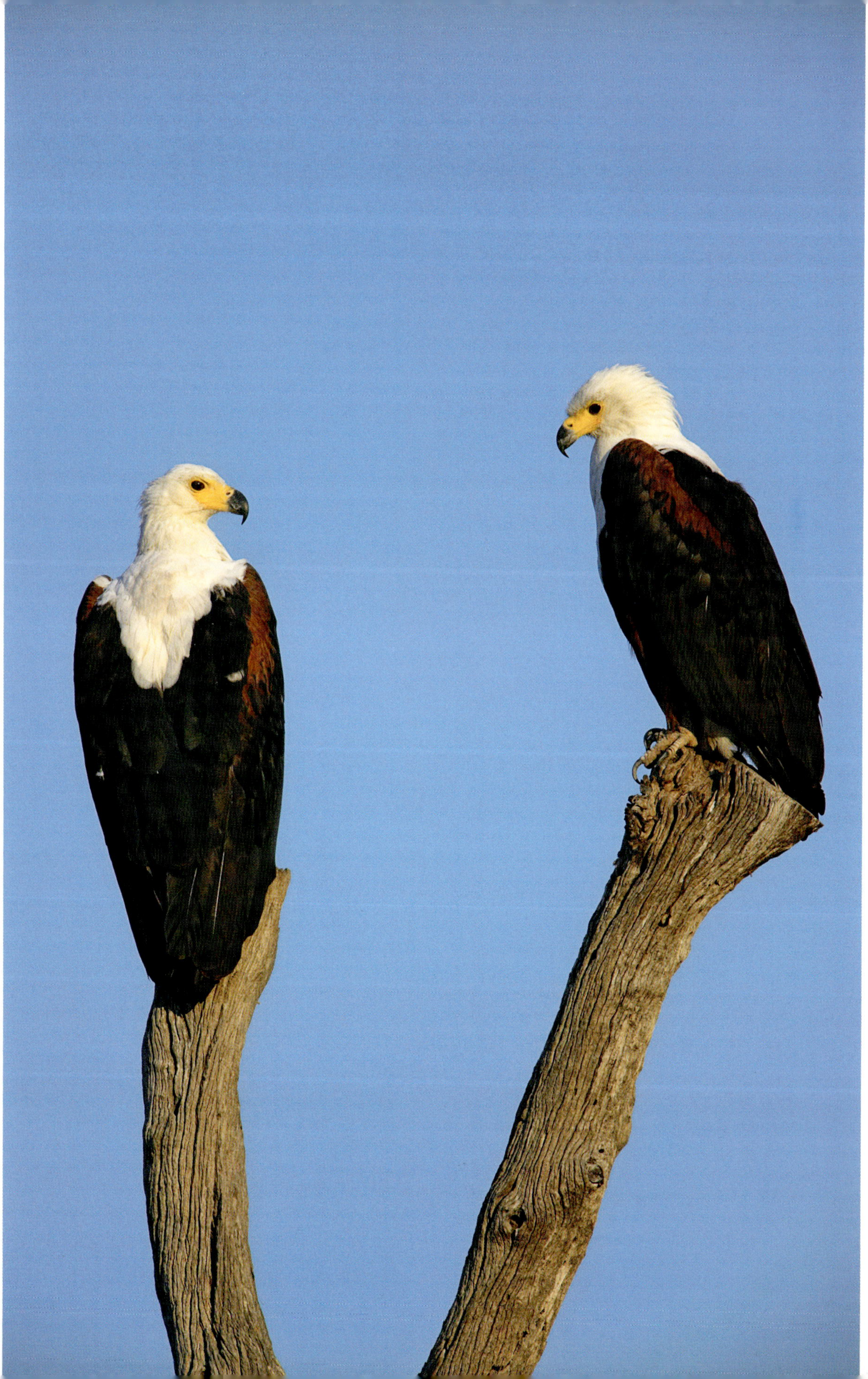

10

WORLD HERITAGE MOUNTAINS

The uKhahlamba-Drakensberg Park is classed a Mixed World Heritage Site, as not only does it preserve unique natural resources, but it protects a rich cultural heritage too. The historically significant San rock art shows diversity of subject matter and creative genius, and provides a window into an ancient culture.

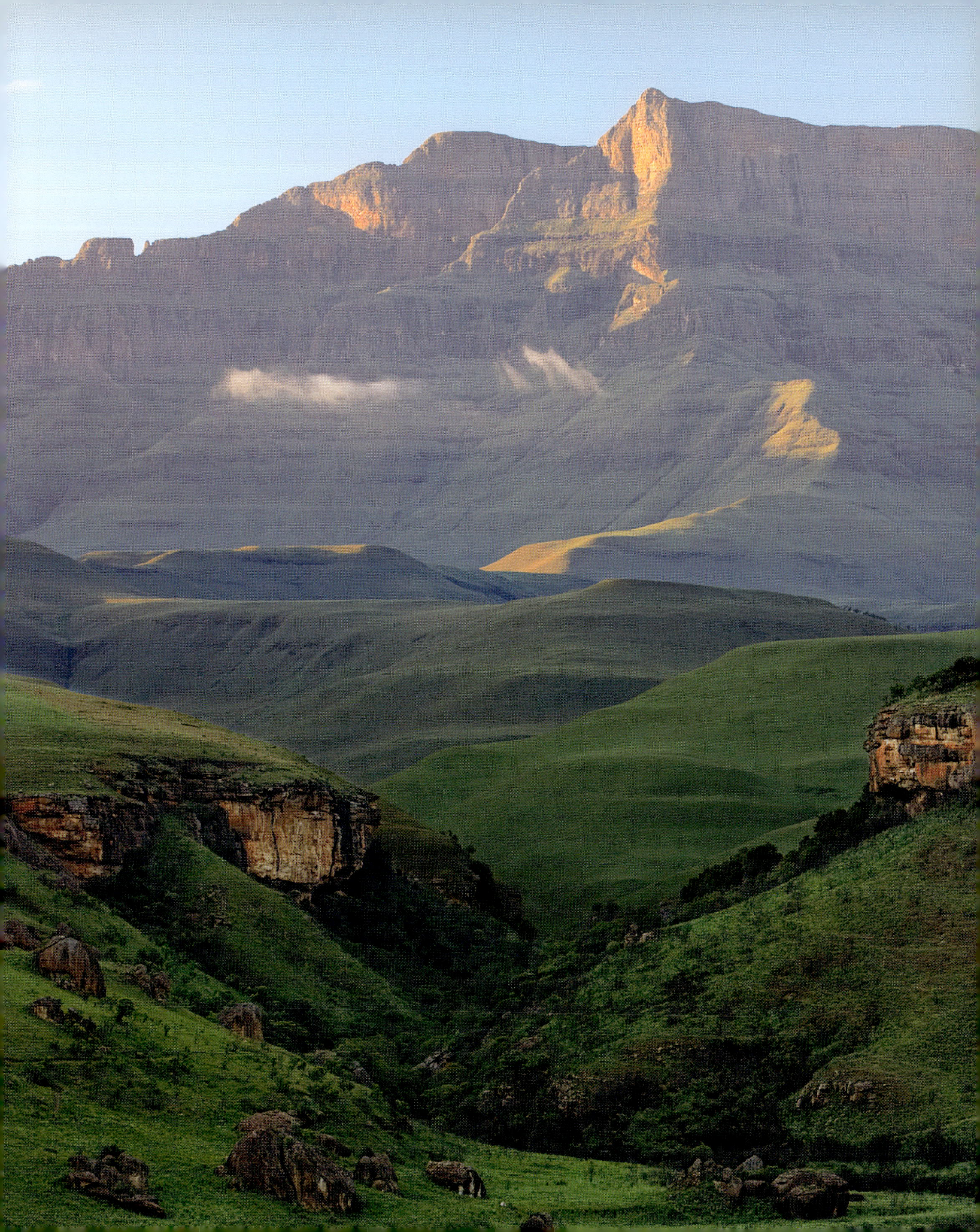

WORLD HERITAGE MOUNTAINS

PREVIOUS PAGE: *The rock faces at Giant's Castle catch the light beautifully.*

OPPOSITE: *There are several walks and hikes along the mountain trails at Lotheni.*

UKHAHLAMBA-DRAKENSBERG PARK

Often called 'the Berg', the Drakensberg ('mountain of the dragons') extends over 500 000 hectares, straddling 300 kilometres of the Lesotho–KZN border. The 243 000-hectare **uKhahlamba-Drakensberg Park** (UDP) combines this Afrikaans name with the Zulu equivalent, meaning 'barrier of spears'.

The World Heritage Convention makes provision for the listing of natural and cultural sites that are unique and have outstanding universal value for all humankind. The UDP, proclaimed a World Heritage Site on 29 December 2000, was established to conserve the globally significant biodiversity of the high mountain escarpment region in South Africa, and to safeguard the water resources essential to this dry country for the benefit of all its people.

The UDP is one of only 25 sites in the world to have been listed as a mixed site – as having both natural and cultural values of outstanding importance. The UDP's rich diversity of plant and animal life, variety of habitats and high-quantity endemic and globally threatened species, especially birds and plants, were considered to be of global value.

Culturally, the historically significant rock paintings made by the San people were lauded. The World Heritage Committee found that the paintings were outstanding both in quality and in diversity of subject matter, which included the depiction of animals and human beings. They also found that these paintings were masterpieces of human creative genius, bearing testimony to the

The Maloti-Drakensberg Transfrontier Conservation and Development Project

Adjacent to the Drakensberg, in the Kingdom of Lesotho, are the Maloti Mountains, known for the exceptional beauty of their natural features. The Maloti-Drakensberg Transfrontier Conservation and Development Project (MDTP) is a collaborative initiative between South Africa and Lesotho to protect the two areas through conservation and sustainable resource and land use.

A great deal of planning has gone into the careful development of both the park and the surrounding areas so that the area can contribute to the livelihoods and wellbeing of its residents, who depend on its resources for thier survival. The park is funded, in part, by the World Bank, and it is administered by Ezemvelo KZN Wildlife.

The isolated nature of the Roof of Africa area, spanning the two countries, makes it a world-class destination for those seeking excitement and adventure combined with solitude and relaxation. Alternatively, visitors may just take the chance to savour the unmatched beauty of one of Earth's last unspoiled places.

At the same time, mountainous areas need to be approached with great respect. Visitors should take the necessary safety precautions as natural phenomena can be unpredictable. It is always wise to be prepared for the worst while enjoying the best.

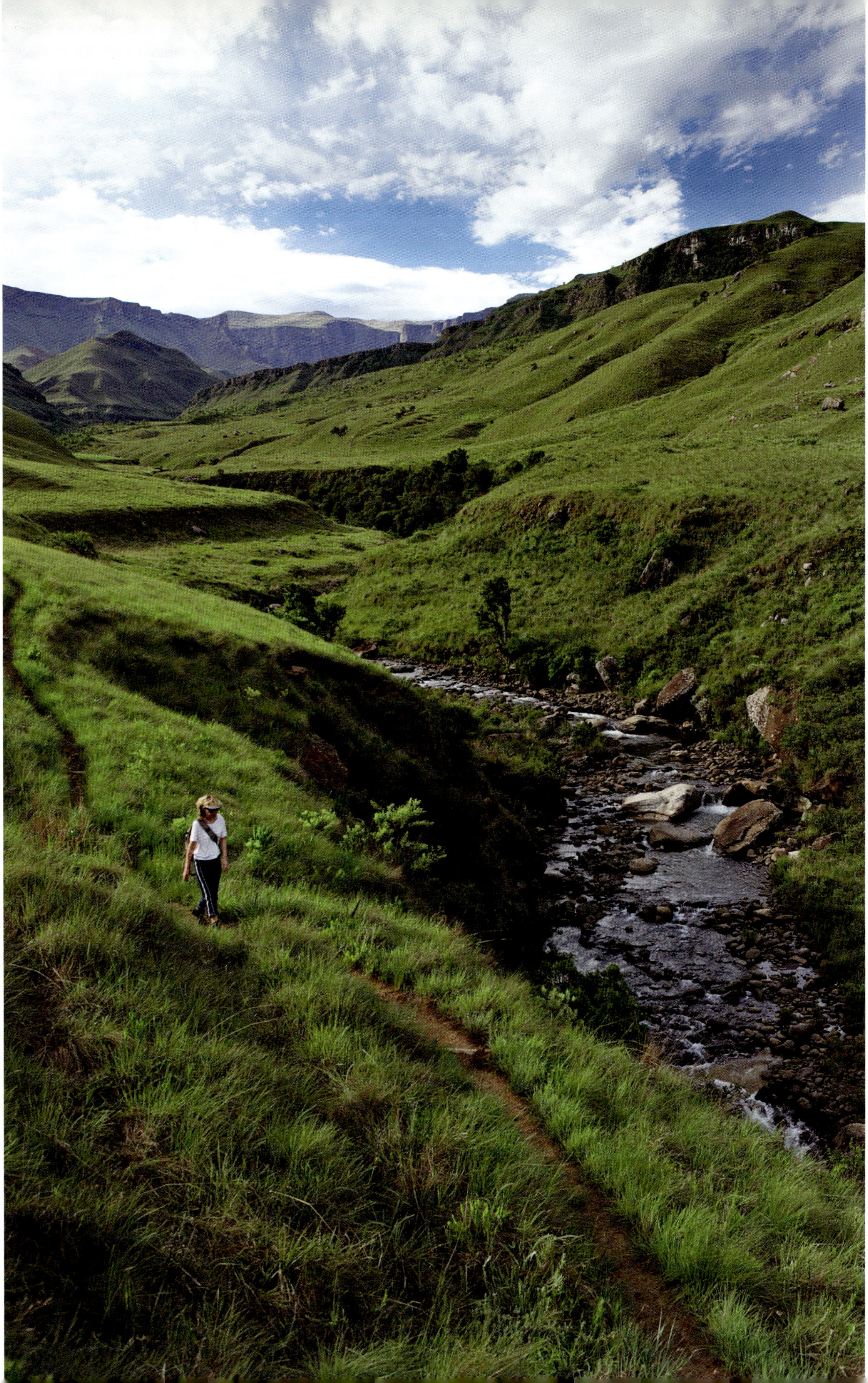

ABOVE: *In winter, the Amphitheatre, as well as many other parts of the uKhahlamba-Drakensberg Park, are covered in snow.*

spiritual life and beliefs of the San people who no longer live in the region. On these grounds the region was declared a Mixed World Heritage Site.

For bookings, the park is administered by **Ezemvelo KZN Wildlife**.

Important biological features

Many species found in the area are listed as endangered. The UDP provides habitats for approximately 2 150 plant species, 60 mammal species, 49 reptile species, 26 amphibian species and 7 fish species. One endemic fish species, the Drakensberg minnow, appears to have disappeared from its stream habitats in South Africa and today is only known to occur in Lesotho.

There are more than 300 bird species in the park. Some 18 species are listed in the South African Red Data Book as threatened species, including the bearded vulture. The mountains also provide nesting and roosting habitats for Cape vulture, and are the strongholds of these birds in Southern Africa.

The park provides a last refuge for herds of eland, of which there are approximately 1 800. The vulnerable oribi antelope and klipspringer occur in the park, as do large numbers of the Southern African endemic grey rhebuck. Of the mammals, there are 11 endemic species in the area.

A few studies suggest a great number of endemic insect species, including planthoppers, crane flies, dance flies and lace wings. The rich diversity includes 33 species of millipedes, 44 species of dragon- and damselflies, 74 species of butterflies and 33 species of predatory robberflies. Remarkably, there is a rich diversity of several groups of ancient forms of insects associated with the high-altitude alpine tundra vegetation, known as paleo-invertebrates.

Two major high-altitude vegetation types exist within the UDP: the higher Austral Afro-alpine vegetation and the lower alti-mountain vegetation, found 2 500 metres above sea level. Approximately 20% of plants are endemic to this region. The entire UDP was listed as a Wetland of International Importance in terms of the Ramsar Convention. The wetlands are considered to be structurally and floristically distinct from all other wetland systems in South Africa. They occur in the highland reaches on both the South African and Lesotho sides of the border and provide a vital hydrological function.

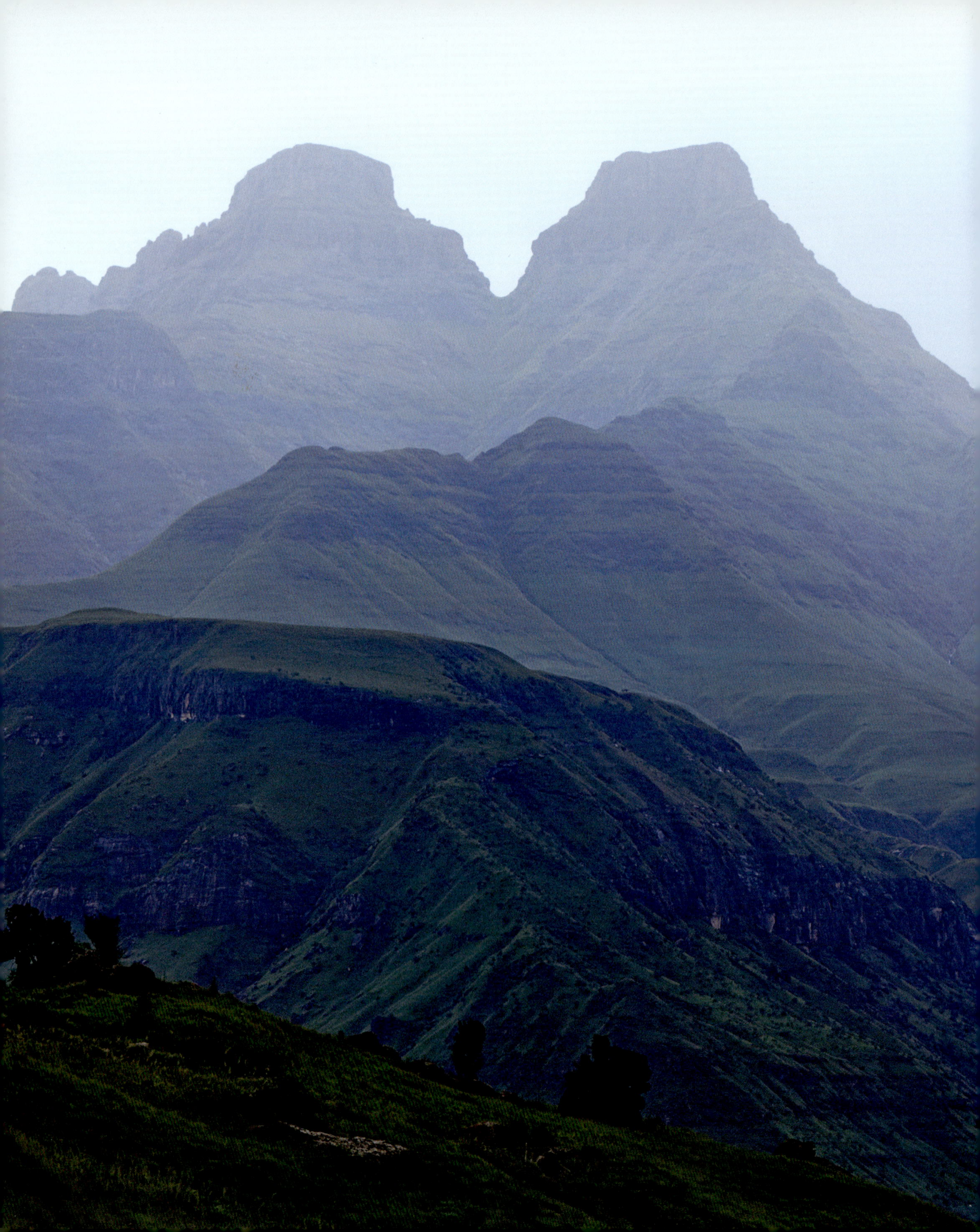

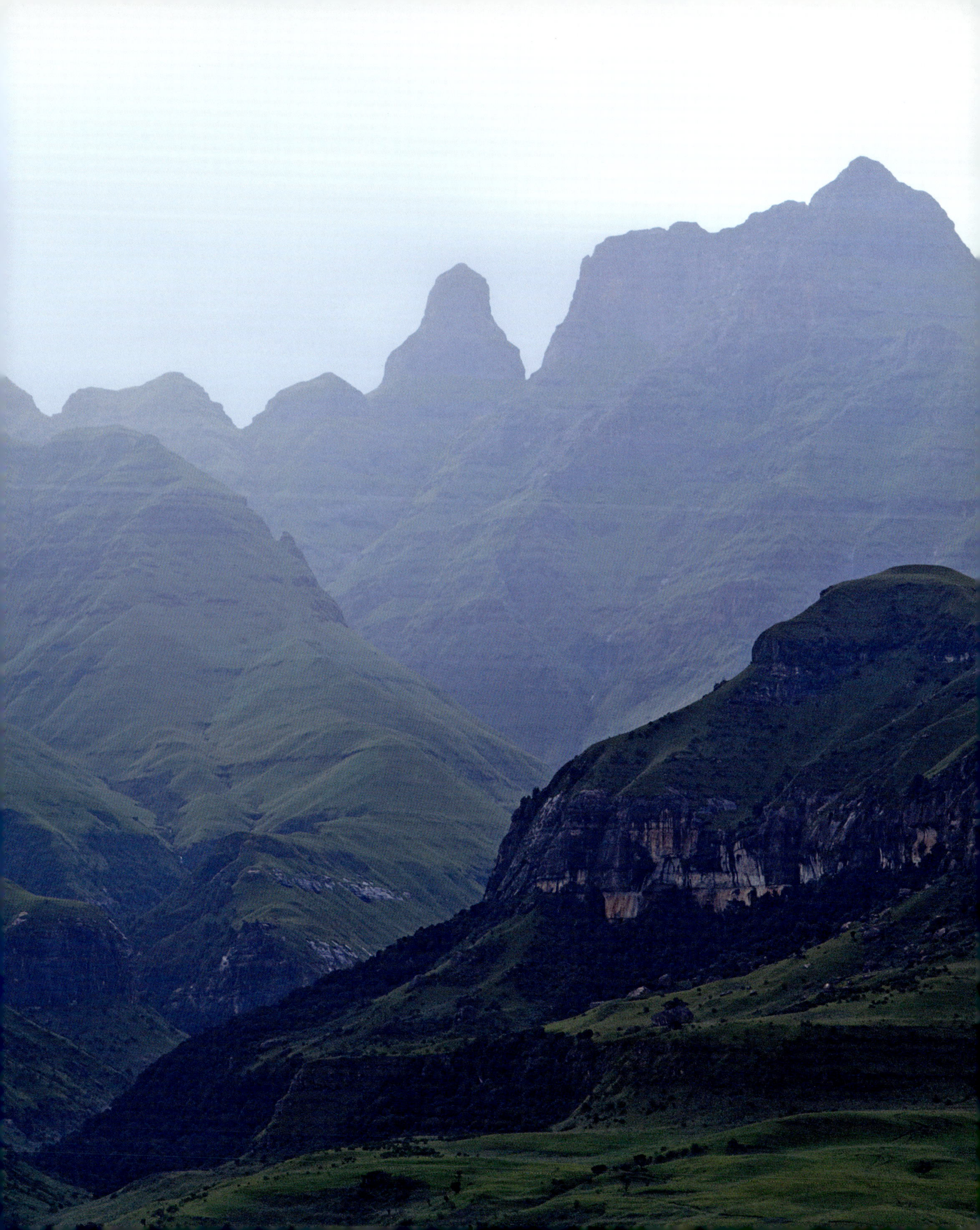

WORLD HERITAGE MOUNTAINS

PREVIOUS PAGES: *Cathedral Peak, in the Central Drakensberg, has some of the most majestic mountain skylines in the uKhahlamba-Drakensberg Park.*

BELOW: *Much of the rock art depicts wild animals such as the eland, with which the San had a great affinity.*

ROCK ART

There are several important areas in Southern Africa containing significant concentrations of San rock art. However, no other area in Africa contains the density and diversity of San rock art as the Maloti-Drakensberg region. There are approximately 600 recorded sites, with 40 000 individual images in the UDP alone, as well as many other sites in the adjacent areas and Lesotho. It is the largest concentrated group of paintings in Africa south of the Sahara and is uniquely different to the rock art found on other continents.

The art represents a very long tradition. The oldest dated painting on a rock shelter is about 2 400 years old, with the more recently painted images created up to the late 19th century.

The paintings and the environment are still just as they were when the last artists lived there. Neither the climate, the vegetation, nor the animals have changed significantly, and in most areas there is very little sign of any human impact.

Most exciting is the possibility of turning from ancient rock paintings of eland, rhebuck or other animals to look out over the pristine valleys, and actually see those very species, still there, on the nearby hillside.

The paintings show a fundamental and deep connection between the San people and nature.

WORLD HERITAGE MOUNTAINS

At the centre of San cosmology is the concept of a spirit world that can be reached by shamans who possess multifaceted supernatural powers. Through trance, these revered shamans cured the sick, made rain, guided antelope towards hunters and even visited the spirit world – an event symbolised by paintings of eland. Interestingly, nearly every rock art shelter contains at least one eland painting, while some have more than 100, many painted one on top of the other, thereby aggregating their spiritual powers and significance.

Apart from images that convey themes of great cultural and spiritual importance, there are others showing historical events and conflicts. Interestingly, there are images of mounted soldiers and sailing ships that must have either been seen by the artists or have been described to them.

Where to see rock art

There are a number of sites in the caves and rock shelters that are open to the public; some of the most accessible and interesting shelters are the **Main Caves** at **Giant's Castle**, just a short half-hour walk from Giant's Castle Main Camp. **Battle Cave** at **Injisuthi** is also easy to reach.

Another wonderful cave is **Game Pass Shelter** at **Kamberg**, but the walk is rather strenuous. An alternative for those who prefer not to make the trek up to the cave is the **Kamberg Rock Art Centre**, where a great video about rock art and the San can be seen. There is another rock art centre at **Didima Camp** at **Cathedral Peak**.

It is not permitted to visit any caves containing rock art without the assistance of a qualified and registered guide. This is not merely to protect the priceless heritage, but also to help visitors with the interpretation and history of the paintings. Having a guide enriches rather than diminishes the experience.

PLACES TO STAY

Royal Natal, in the northern Drakensberg, was proclaimed a protected area in 1916. A highlight of the park is the **Tugela Falls**, where the river alternately follows and plummets down an approximately 5-kilometre-long, 500-metre-high

WORLD HERITAGE MOUNTAINS

RIGHT: *Didima Camp, with its thatch cottages that bring hobbits to mind, is one of the many beautiful camps situated within the park.*

OPPOSITE: *The Tugela Falls tumble off the edge of the iconic Amphitheatre in the north of uKhahlamba-Drakensberg Park.*

gorge. The falls themselves total some 850 metres, making them the highest in the country.

Thendele Camp, with views of the world-famous Amphitheatre from each chalet, is situated closer than any other to the main escarpment and has the distinction of being Ezemvelo KZN Wildlife's most popular camp. Trout fishing is prized at the two dams and in the Mahai and uThukela rivers. This is one of the only places where horse-riding is allowed.

Didima Camp in the Central Drakensberg has hobbit-style chalets, a San Art Interpretive Centre with audiovisual displays, state-of-the-art conference facilities, a swimming pool and tennis courts. At the central lodge is a restaurant and bar, shop and fireside lounge. Walk or take a guided drive up Mike's Pass to the top of the Little Drakensberg, near the head of the Didima Gorge.

Monk's Cowl is the access point for the **Mdedelelo Wilderness Area** and is ideal for camping, walks to Sterkspruit Falls, Nandi Falls and the gorge, or a more adventurous hike up Ship's Prow Pass to Inkosazana Cave on Champagne Castle. The rock pools are great for swimming.

Injisuthi takes its name, meaning 'the dog has eaten sufficiently', from the days when there was plentiful game in the area for everyone. The

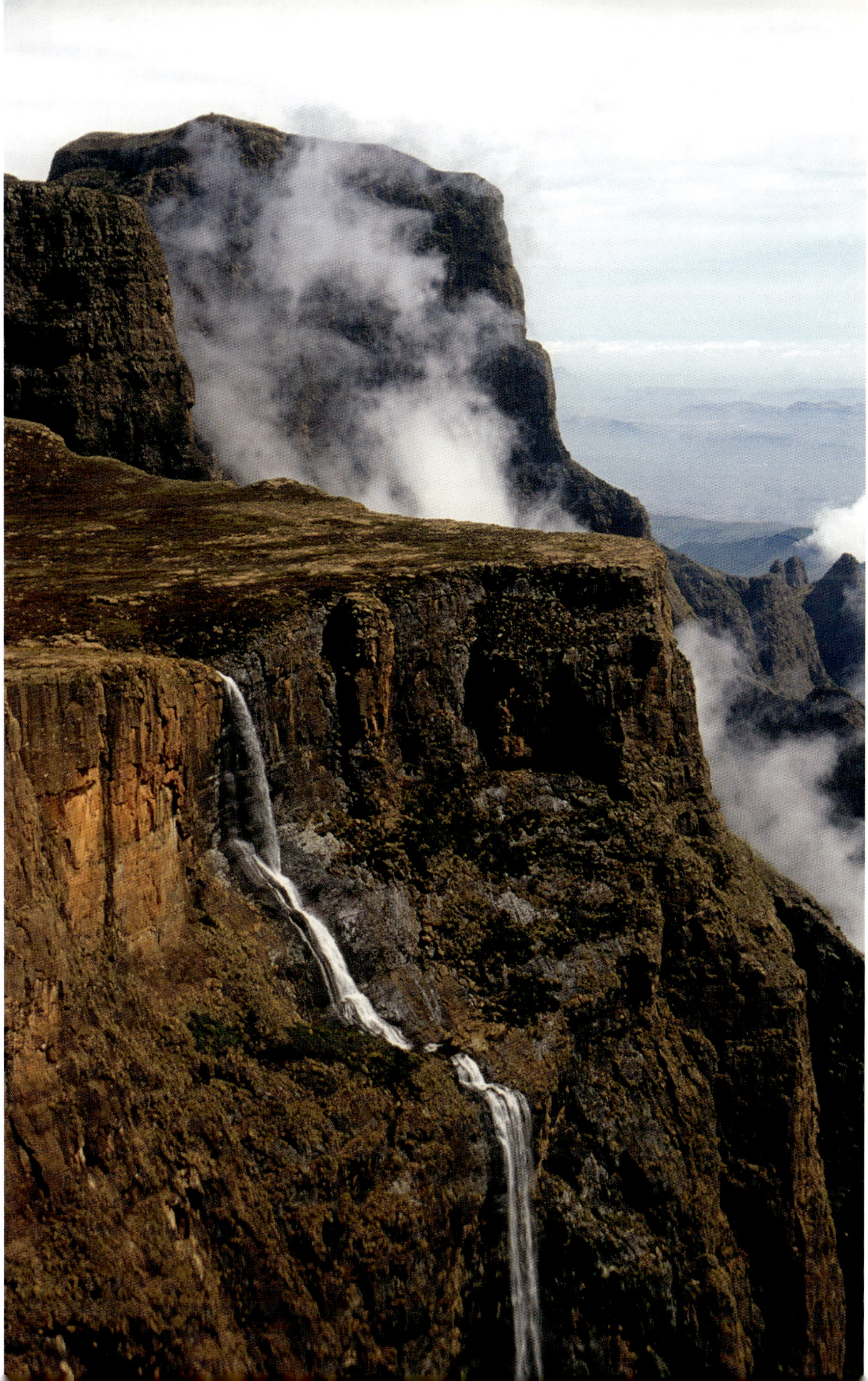

WORLD HERITAGE MOUNTAINS

BELOW: *Many camps, such as at Giant's Castle, tucked into the mountainside, offer great views of the escarpment from their verandahs.*

BELOW RIGHT: *Rivers and streams run off the mountainsides throughout the uKhahlamba-Drakensberg Park.*

OPPOSITE: *Rainbow Gorge near Cathedral Peak is known for its beautiful waterfalls, and the rainbows created when the sunlight shines through their spray.*

mountains which backdrop this reserve are Cathkin Peak, Monk's Cowl and Champagne Castle, and there are beautiful hikes, self-contained cottages, cabins and a very pretty camp site.

Giant's Castle Camp is situated in a 40-year-old indigenous garden. This is a good starting point for hikes into the mountains and for overnighting in tents or caves. The Main Caves, with their unique rock art panels, are an easy 30-minute walk away. There are guided tours twice daily for a small fee. From May to September this also the place to view the rare bearded vulture. Advance booking is essential.

The Southern Drakensberg's popular **Kamberg Nature Reserve**, named after a nearby mountain resembling a rooster's comb (*kam* in Afrikaans), has an excellent rock art centre and great walks to view rock art nearby. With the Mooi River flowing through it, there is also fantastic trout fishing in the area.

The pretty hutted camp of **Loteni** offers hikes with the possibility of seeing mountain antelope, Cape clawless otter and other wild animals. Mountain biking is allowed in designated areas and swimming in the Cool Pools is fantastic. Some 16 kilometres of the Loteni River is stocked with brown trout. The small Settlers' Homestead Museum is located nearby.

Garden Castle is where the **Giant's Cup Hiking Trail** starts. Three of the five overnight huts are in the reserve and there are several caves where hikers can overnight. A challenging climb is up Rhino Peak, which culminates at a somewhat exhausting 3 051 metres above sea level.

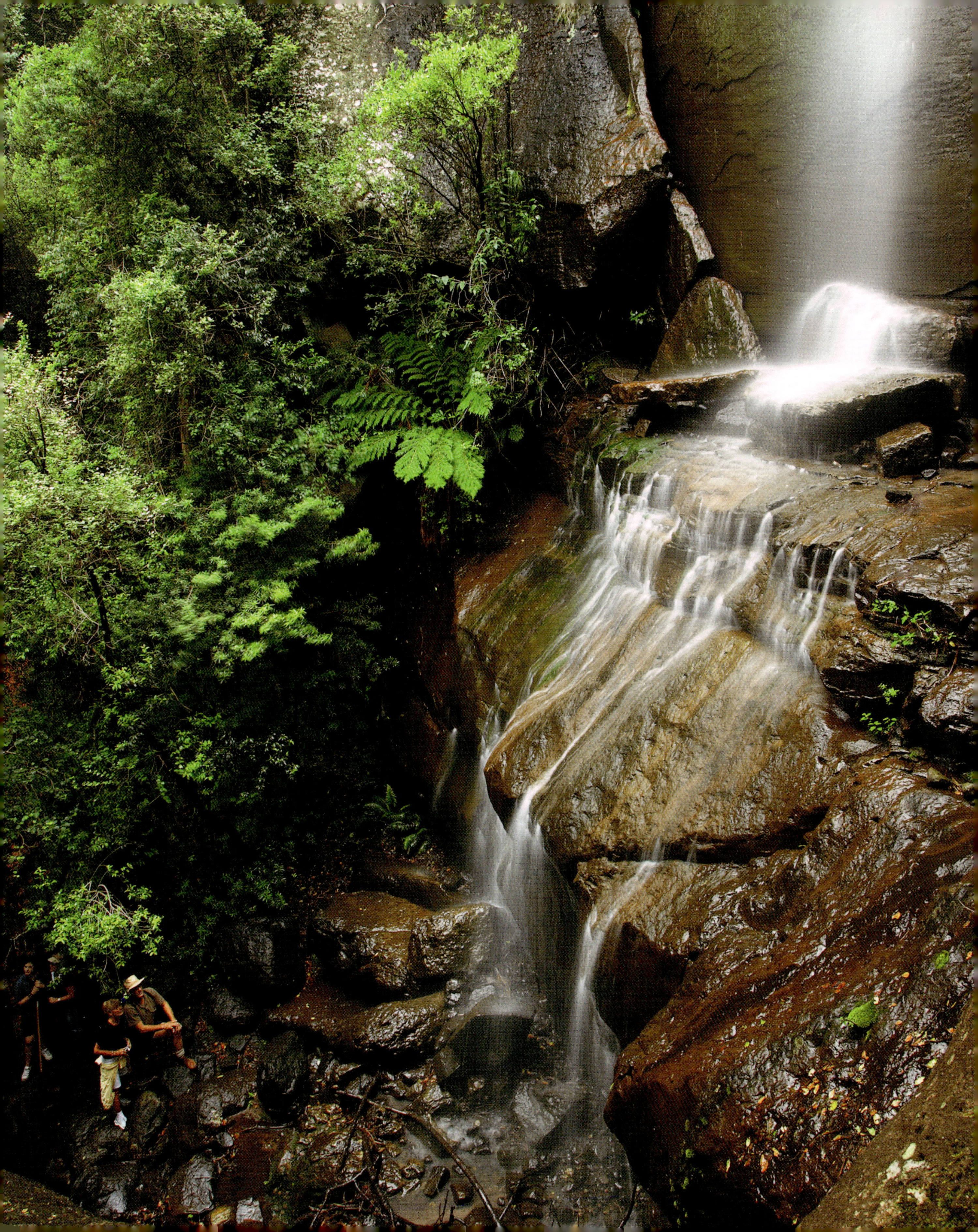

ABOVE: *Visitors to Giant's Castle, high in the mountains, are rewarded with breathtaking views.*

THINGS TO DO
Arts and crafts

Heading towards the Central Drakensberg area through Champagne Valley, drivers will pass a number of artists' studios, craft shops, tea gardens and restaurants. **Thokozisa Lifestyle Centre**, at the R600 crossroads, is where San-style crafts, organic herb products, music, clothing and home-made farm goodies can be bought. Visitors can also get information about the region and have a light lunch at the coffee shop.

Set far up in the mountains, **Falcon Ridge Birds of Prey Display Centre** is one of the most popular venues in Champagne Valley. There are two shows daily (apart from Friday) in which a variety of birds of prey are showcased, such as lanner falcon, peregrine falcon, and black, crowned and African hawk eagles.

A visit to the region would not be complete without attending a concert by the world-famous **Drakensberg Boys' Choir**, held every Wednesday afternoon throughout the term.

A fantastic option for 4x4 enthusiasts is the eco-ethnic historical tour to 'the top of the world' in Lesotho in the Southern Drakensberg, via **Sani Pass**. Once there, visitors can have a late lunch or early sundowners at the **Sani Top Chalet** while enjoying the magnificent views. At 2 874 metres it is said to house the highest pub in Africa. The border between Lesotho and South Africa closes late afternoon, so to watch the sun rise or set, book into the lodge to stay overnight.

Take warm clothes in winter – it snows up there! As travellers will exit South Africa and enter Lesotho, passports are required.

Hiking paths and caves

To enjoy the scenery while hiking or walking is one of the predominant reasons people visit the UDP and there are some 1 800 kilometres of well-planned paths throughout the park to accommodate this. As this is a wilderness area it is quite a job to keep these trails maintained. The landscape has steep slopes, high seasonal rainfall, shallow soils, regular fires and vegetation that is slow to recover.

The risk of soil erosion is high. Paths, used for both recreational and management activities are, in fact, one of the biggest erosion hazards in this mountainous catchment environment. Therefore it bodes well if hikers keep to the trails provided for both safety reasons and for the sake of the soil, and do not walk next to the paths or make any paths of their own.

There are hiking trails and walks to suit all requirements and levels of fitness. **Giant's Cup** at Cobham is a three-, four- or five-day trail (just less than 60 kilometres) and is one of the most popular

ABOVE: *Royal Natal has wonderful walks and hikes for people of all ages and fitness levels.*

WORLD HERITAGE MOUNTAINS

BELOW: *Paper hearts are just one of the many beautiful and delicate wild flowers seen on the hillsides after spring rains.*

OPPOSITE LEFT: *One of the few places to see bearded vultures is in the uKhahlamba-Drakensberg Park.*

OPPOSITE RIGHT: *The views from the top of Sani Pass are a worthwhile reward for the adventurous.*

in the Drakensberg, giving hikers a variety of experiences through truly beautiful landscapes.

Another popular trail is the **uThukela Gorge** in Royal Natal, a mere 7-odd kilometres, taking 2-odd hours, which includes views of the spectacular Amphitheatre, a wall of rock more than 2 900 metres high and 4 000 metres wide. The trail is situated between the 3 047-metre-high Eastern Buttress, the 3 121-metre-high South and Beacon buttresses and the 3 165-metre high Sentinel in the north.

Fires

The ecosystems of the Drakensberg have evolved with fire, and as well as being a natural phenomenon it is an important conservation management tool. Considerable effort goes into planning burning programmes and allocating resources for fire protection, but there are still many challenges related to uncontrolled fire.

To get animals to move where they would like them to, cattle rustlers, poachers and others light fires, which can be extremely difficult to control. Several long-term experiments have been set up to better understand the role and impacts of fire on both vegetation and animals in the region.

The uThukela River plummets over **Mont-Aux-Sources**, plunging some 850 metres off the plateau in a series of five stunning waterfalls, far down into the gorge below. It is possible to hike right to the bottom of the Amphitheatre in about six hours. For the more adventurous, try the thrilling **Cathedral Peak Trail** that offers an experienced hiker the opportunity to ascend one of the major freestanding peaks in the UDP.

There are a number of caves, overhead shelters and smaller, more intimate shelters in which to overnight. However, always take a tent along in case bad weather prevents arrival at the destined shelter. Sleeping in caves with rock art is prohibited. Booking through Ezemvelo KZN Wildlife or AMAFA is essential.

Bearded vultures

One of the few places in Africa where there are opportunities to see the bearded vulture is in the Maloti-Drakensberg region. Due to the decline in numbers, much research is planned in order to better protect and preserve these endangered birds. Researchers in South Africa and Lesotho are collaborating with scientists in both Europe and Ethiopia, the only other African country with a viable breeding population.

The birds are threatened by loss of food in the form of appropriate carcasses, electrocution on high power lines, poisoning by ill-informed farmers and the traditional medicine market. The best places to see bearded vultures is at one of the managed 'vulture restaurants' within UDP or at Lammergeier Hide in the **Lammergeier Private Nature Reserve**, but due to their scarcity a sighting can obviously not be guaranteed.

A trip will not be wasted, however, as lanner falcon, jackal buzzards, Cape vultures and black eagles are likely to be seen.

Fly-fishing

Fly-fishing is popular in the rivers and streams in UDP and the surrounding areas. Wild spawn trout found in the faster-flowing streams are smaller than those stocked in dams and are fit and wily, offering a nice challenge for fishermen. Kamberg and Loteni have great trout fishing and there is an annual trout festival in May.

The Southern Drakensberg around Underberg also has good trout fishing waters as well as dams stocked with bass. Yellowfish can be caught in the lower reaches of the rivers.

CONTACT DETAILS

GENERAL

AMAFA
☎ Head office 035 870 2050/1/2
☎ Pietermaritzburg 033 394 6543
⌂ www.heritagekzn.co.za

eThekwini Municipality
☎ 031 311 1111
⌂ www.durban.gov.za

Ezemvelo KZN Wildlife
☎ Information 033 845 1999
☎ Reservations 033 845 1000
⌂ www.kznwildlife.com

KZN Tourism
Tourist Junction Building, 3rd Floor, 160 Monty Naicker Rd (former Pine St), Durban ☎ 031 366 7500 or 0860 101 099 ⌂ www.zulu.org.za

World Wide Fund For Nature South Africa (WWF-SA)
☎ 021 888 2800 or 011 262 9460
⌂ www.wwfsa.org.za

THE PEOPLE

Annual Royal Reed Dance
☎ 035 474 4919 or 082 492 6918

Baynesfield Estate
Near Richmond ☎ 033 251 0559
⌂ www.baynesfieldmuseum.co.za

Cool Runnings
49 Milne St, Durban
☎ 031 368 5604 or 084 701 6912
⌂ www.coolrunnings.co.za

DumaZulu Lodge & Traditional Village
Near Hluhluwe ☎ 035 562 0353

Durban Cultural and Documentation Centre
Cnr Epsom Rd and Derby St, Durban ☎ 031 309 7559

Emnambithi Cultural Centre
NGR Building, Muchasen St, Ladysmith ☎ 036 635 4231

Fugitives Drift Lodge
Rorke's Drift ☎ 034 642 1843 or 034 271 8051
⌂ www.fugitives-drift-lodge.com

Isandlwana Lodge
Isandlwana off R68
☎ 034 271 8301
⌂ www.isandlwana.co.za

Killie Campbell Museum
220 Gladys Mazibuko Rd (former Marriott Rd), Durban
☎ 031 260 1720
⌂ www.campbell.ukzn.ac.za

PheZulu Safari Park
Old Main Rd (R103), Botha's Hill
☎ 031 777 1000/1464
⌂ www.phezulusafaripark.co.za

Shakaland
Near eShowe off R66
☎ 035 460 0912
⌂ www.shakaland.com

SpionKop Lodge
Near Ladysmith off R600
☎ 036 488 1404
⌂ www.spionkop.co.za

FAITHS OF THE PEOPLE

SanAquam Urban Ayurvedic Spa
Level 1, Kensington Blvd, 54 Adelaide Tambo Dr (former Kensington Dr), Durban North
☎ 0861 999 181
⌂ www.sanaquamayurvedicspa.com

Buddhist Retreat Centre
D64, iXopo ☎ 039 834 1863
⌂ www.brcixopo.co.za

Centekow Mission
Off R612, Creighton
☎ 039 833 0033
⌂ www.centocowmission.org

Church of the Vow
Voortrekker/Msunduzi Museum, 351 Langalibalele St, Pietermaritzburg
☎ 033 394 6834/5/6
⌂ www.voortrekkermuseum.co.za

Durban Jewish Club
44 KE Masinga Rd (former Old Fort Rd), Durban ☎ 031 335 4450
⌂ www.djc.co.za

Hazrath Soofie Saheb Masjid
Soofie Saheb Dr, Riverside, Durban
☎ 031 564 5051
⌂ www.soofie.saheb.org.za

Holocaust Centre
44 KE Masinga Rd (former Old Fort Rd), Durban ☎ 031 368 6833 or 031 335 4461 ⌂ www.djc.co.za

Jummah Mosque
Dr Yusuf Dadoo St (former Grey St), Durban ☎ 031 304 1518

King's Grant Country Retreat
☎ 039 834 2730
⌂ www.kingsgrant.co.za

Kwasizabantu Mission
R74, about 50km from both Stanger and Greytown
☎ 032 481 5727
⌂ www.kwasizabantu.com

Lourdes Mission
Near Umzimkulu ☎ Diocese of Umzimkulu 039 433 1421

Maria Ratschitz Mission
Wasbank, Dundee
☎ 034 651 1722

Mariannhill Monastery
10 Monastery Rd, Mariannhill, Durban ☎ 031 700 4288
⌂ www.mariannhillmonastery.co.za

Mariathal Mission
R56, iXopo ☎ 039 834 1843

Richenau Mission
Underberg ☎ 033 701 1891/1202

Sri Ambalavanaar Alayam Temple
890 Bellair Rd, Cato Manor, Durban
☎ 031 261 5030

Sri Ganesha Temple
Siphosetu Rd, Mount Edgecombe
☎ 031 539 3409

Sri Jagannath Puri Temple
Tongaat
☎ Contact AMAFA

Sri Mariamman Temple
Old Main Rd, Isipingo Rail

Sri Muruga Kadaval Temple
152 Jacobs Rd, Jacobs, Durban

Sri Sri Radhanath Temple of Understanding
50 Bhaktivedanta Swami Circle, Chatsworth, Durban
☎ 031 403 3328

Woza Moya Project
☎ 072 193 3945
⌂ www.wozamoya.org.za

Zululand Eco Adventures
☎ 035 474 4919
⌂ www.eshowe.com

CREATIVE THINKING

1000 Hills Craft Village
Old Main Rd, Drummond, Valley of a Thousand Hills ☎ 031 777 1189 or 083 942 0886

Africa Centre for Health and Population Studies
Umkhanyakude district
☎ 0800 203 695 or 035 550 7500
⌂ www.africacentre.ac.za

The African Art Centre
94 Florida Rd, Durban
☎ 031 312 3804/5
⌂ www.afriart.org.za

Amandla Beadwork
Zulu Reserve Rd, Botha's Hill, Valley of a Thousand Hills
☎ 031 777 1104 or 083 880 1383

Ardmore Ceramic Art
Off N3, Caversham, Midlands
☎ 033 234 4869
⌂ www.ardmoreceramics.co.za

Art in the Park
Alexandra Park, Chief Albert Luthuli Rd (former Commercial Rd), Pietermaritzburg ☎ 033 345 1348
⌂ www.artinthepark.co.za

artSPACE
3 Millar Rd, Stamford Hill, Durban
☎ 031 312 0793
⌂ www.artspace-durban.com

The Barnyard Theatre
Shop F222, Gateway, uMhlanga Ridge, Durban ☎ 031 566 3045
⌂ www.barnyardtheatre.co.za

BAT Centre
45 Maritime Place, Small Craft Harbour, Durban ☎ 031 332 0451
⌂ www.batcentre.co.za

Bauchop
Paul Kruger Ave, Palm Beach
☎ 039 313 5998
⌂ www.kwikwap.co.za/bauchop

Beatrice Street YMCA
Charlotte Maxeke St (former Beatrice St), Durban
☎ 084 927 6477

Born in Africa
Balgowan, Midlands
☎ 033 234 4796
⌂ www.borninafrica.co.za

CONTACT DETAILS

Boswells Building
74 Gladstone St, Dundee
☎ 033 394 6543

Cafe Vacca Matta
Shop U4, Suncoast Casino & Entertainment World, 20 Battery Beach Rd, North Beach, Durban
☎ 031 368 6535

The Candle Dipping Shop
Nottingham Road, Midlands
☎ 033 266 6980
www.candledippingshop.com

Catalina Theatre
18 Boatman's Rd, Wilson's Wharf, Durban
☎ 031 309 7945 or 031 305 6889
www.catalinatheatre.co.za

The Centre for Jazz and Popular Music
Francis Stock Building, Howard College Campus, Durban
☎ 031 260 2377

Drakensberg Boys' Choir
Winterton ☎ 036 468 1012
www.dbchoir.info

Dockyard Supper Theatre
Shop 221, Musgrave Centre, 115 Musgrave Rd, Berea, Durban
☎ 031 332 1086
www.dockyardtheatre.co.za

Durban Art Deco Society
☎ 031 301 1951 or 031 266 3082
www.durbandeco.org.za

Durban Art Gallery
City Hall, Anton Lembede St (former Smith St), Durban
☎ 031 311 2264/9

Durban University of Technology Gallery
Cecil Renaud Theatre, 2nd floor, Steve Biko Campus ☎ 031 373 2207

Eden On Essenwood
199 Stephen Dlamini Rd (former Essenwood Rd), Durban
☎ 031 201 9176

Elizabeth Sneddon Theatre
University of KZN, Howard College Campus, Mazisi Kunene Rd (former King George V Ave/South Ridge Rd), Glenwood ☎ 031 260 2296
www.sneddontheatre.co.za

Glass Cuttings Shop and Gallery
Hilton, Midlands
☎ 033 343 2088

Groundcover Leather Company
Off N3, halfway between Mooi River and Pietermaritzburg, Midlands ☎ 033 330 6092
www.groundcover.co.za

The Hexagon Theatre
University of KZN, Pietermaritzburg
☎ 033 260 5537
www.hexagon.ukzn.ac.za

Hilton Arts Festival
Hilton College Theatre, Hilton, Midlands, ☎ 033 383 0126

Hi-Fly Kites
D795, Merrivale, Midlands
☎ 033 330 5746
www.hiflykites.co.za

Hillcrest Aids Centre & Craft Shop
26 Old Main Rd, Hillcrest, Durban
☎ 031 765 5866 or 073 237 5522

Johnson Bros Country Furniture
The Rotunda, Hilton, Midlands
☎ 033 394 1801
www.johnsonbros.co.za

KZNSA Gallery
166 Bulwer Rd, Glenwood, Durban
☎ 031 277 1705
www.nsagallery.co.za

The Lavender Co.
D666 near Dargle, Midlands
☎ 033 234 4741

Lona's Pianos
114 off the N3, Lions River, Midlands
☎ 033 234 4343/37
www.pianos.co.za

Midlands Meander
☎ Office 033 330 8195
Helpline en route 082 231 0042
www.midlandsmeander.co.za

Ondini Historical Complex
King Cetshwayo Highway, uLundi
☎ 035 870 2051
www.heritagekzn.co.za

Playhouse Theatre Complex
231 Anton Lembede St (former Smith St), Durban
☎ 031 369 9555
www.playhousecompany.com

Rainbow Restaurant
Shop 6, 23 Stanfield Ln, Pinetown
☎ 031 702 9161
www.therainbow.co.za

The Rhumbelow Theatre
The Rhumbelow Shellhole, Cunningham Rd (off Bartle Rd), Umbilo
☎ 031 205 7602 or 082 499 8636
www.rhumbelow.za.net

Rotunda Farm Stall
1 Cedara Road, Hilton, Midlands
☎ 033 343 4205

Shuttleworth Weavers
10km from Nottingham Road, Fort Nottingham, Midlands
☎ 033 266 6818
www.shuttleworthweaving.com

Spiral Blue
Between Lions River and Lidgetton, Midlands
☎ 033 234 4799 or 072 513 0427

Splashy Fen
Splashy Fen Farm Rd, off D600 near Underberg ☎ 031 563 0824
www.splashyfen.co.za

Tatham Art Gallery
Chief Albert Luthuli Rd (former Commercial Rd), opposite City Hall, Pietermaritzburg
☎ 033 392 2800/1
www.tatham.org.za

Thunder Road Rock Diner
136 Florida Rd, Morningside, Durban ☎ 031 303 3440
www.thunderroaddiner.co.za

Voortrekker/Msunduzi Museum
351 Langalibalele St, Pietermaritzburg
☎ 033 394 6834/5/6
www.voortrekkermuseum.co.za

The Weaver's Hut
Howick, Midlands
☎ 033 330 4399 or 082 964 5363
www.weavershut.com

Yossi's Café
127 Davenport Road, Glenwood, Durban ☎ 031 201 0090

Zulu Jazz Lounge
231 Anton Lembede (former Smith St), Durban ☎ 031 304 2377

PLAYING GAMES

Air Safaris
Virginia Airport, Durban
☎ 084 257 0835
www.airandoceansafaris.co.za

Amashovashova
Pietermaritzburg/Durban
☎ 031 312 8896
www.amashova.co.za

Beach and Bush
Unit M03, uShaka Marine World, Mahatma Gandhi Rd (former Point Rd) Durban
☎ 031 266 9221/5120
www.beachandbush.co.za

Blue Sky
Cato Ridge Airfield ☎ 031 765 1318
www.blusky.co.za

Champagne Sports Resort
Central Drakensberg
☎ 036 468 8000
www.champagnesportsresort.com

Comrades Marathon
Pietermaritzburg/Durban
☎ 033 897 8650
www.comrades.com

Cool Runnings
49 Milne St, Durban
☎ 031 368 5604 or 084 701 6912
www.coolrunnings.co.za

Cyclone Extreme Products
25 Hunter St, Durban
☎ 031 368 6864
www.cyclonekiteboarding.com

Drakensberg Canopy Tour
☎ 036 468 1981 or 083 661 5691
www.drakensbergcanopytour.co.za

Durban Country Club
101 Isaiah Ntshangase Rd (former Walter Gilbert Rd), Durban
☎ 031 313 1777
www.dcclub.co.za

Durban July
Greyville Racecourse, 150 Avondale Rd, Greyville, Durban ☎ 031 314 1500
www.vodacomdurbanjuly.co.za

Dusi Canoe Marathon
Pietermaritzburg/Durban
☎ 033 394 9994 or 033 342 1528
www.dusi.org.za

CONTACT DETAILS

Fardoun Spa
Nottingham Road, Midlands
☎ 033 266 6217
🌐 www.fordoun.com

Giant's Castle Mountain Bike Challenge
Giant's Castle, Drakensberg
🌐 www.ecomotion.co.za

iMfolozi Big 5 MTB Challenge
Hluhluwe-iMfolozi Park
🌐 www.imfolozimtb.co.za

Jeep uShaka Surf and Adventure Centre
uShaka Beach, in front of uShaka Marine World, Durban
☎ 084 823 9470
🌐 www.surfandadventures.co.za

JNC Helicopter Tours
Hangar 1, Virginia Airport, Durban
☎ 031 563 9513
🌐 www.jncheli.co.za

Joe Cool's
Durban Beachfront ☎ 031 332 9697
🌐 www.joecools.co.za

Karkloof Canopy Tours
Karkloof Nature Reserve, Midlands
☎ 033 330 3415 or 076 241 2888
🌐 www.karkloofcanopytour.co.za

Karkloof Classic Mountain Bike Festival
Karkloof, Midlands
🌐 www.karkloofclassic.co.za

Karkloof Spa Wellness & Wildlife Retreat
Ihlanze Ranch, Otto's Bluff Rd, Cramond, Pietermaritzburg
☎ 033 569 1321
🌐 www.karkloofspa.com

Midmar Mile
Midmar Dam, Midmar, Midlands
☎ 0861 643 627
🌐 www.midmarmile.co.za

Mr Price Pro
🌐 www.mrpricepro.com

Peak High Mountaineering
☎ 033 343 3168
🌐 www.peakhigh.co.za

Prince's Grant
Off R102, Dukuza, North Coast
☎ 032 482 0002
🌐 www.princesgrant.co.za

San Lameer
Off N2 near Margate, South Coast
☎ 039 313 5141
Villa rentals 039 313 0450
🌐 www.sanlameer.co.za

Selbourne
Off N2 near Pennington
☎ 039 688 1896
🌐 www.selborne.com

Sharks Ticket Office
12 Isaiah Ntshangase Rd (former Walter Gilbert Rd) Durban
☎ 031 308 8502
🌐 www.sharksrugby.co.za

Skydive Durban
Pietermaritzburg Airport
☎ 072 214 6040
🌐 www.skydivedurban.co.za

Skyguide Paragliding
54 Westville Road, Westville, Durban ☎ 031 266 5774 or 082 904 1020

St Lucia Kayak Safaris
St Lucia ☎ 035 590 1233 or 082 463 3253
🌐 www.kayaksafaris.co.za

South Coast Helicopter Services
South Coast ☎ 039 315 6427 or 082 781 2491/2

uShaka Marine World
1 Bell St, Durban
☎ 031 328 8000
🌐 www.ushakamarineworld.co.za

Wave House
Shop G83, Gateway Theatre of Shopping, uMhlanga Ridge
☎ 031 584 9400
🌐 www.wavehouse.co.za

Wild 5
Oribi Gorge Hotel, off N2 near Port Shepstone
☎ 039 687 0253
🌐 www.oribigorge.co.za

Wild Coast Sun Country Club
Main Bizana Rd (R61), Wild Coast Sun Hotel, Port Edward
☎ 039 305 9111/2799

Zero Four Flight School
Margate Airport, Margate
☎ 039 317 4348
🌐 www.fly margate.co.za

Zimbali
M4, uMhlali
☎ 032 538 1041
🌐 www.zimbali.co.za

FOOD AND DRINK

Aubergine & Andreotti's
Old Main Rd, Hillcrest, Durban
☎ 031 765 6050

Banana Café and Pancake House
R61 between Palm Beach and Munster ☎ 039 319 1454
🌐 www.macbanana.co.za

Britannia Hotel
1299 Umgeni Rd, Durban
☎ 031 303 2266/2417
🌐 www.hotelbrits.co.za

Café 1999
Shop 2, Silvervause Centre, 11 Vause Rd, Musgrave, Durban
☎ 031 202 3406
🌐 www.cafe1999.co.za

Café Bloom
R103 Old Main Rd, Nottingham Road, Midlands ☎ 033 266 6118

Caversham Mill Restaurant
Balgowan, Midlands
☎ 033 234 4524
🌐 www.cavershammill.co.za

Cleopatra Mountain Farmhouse
Balgowan, Midlands
☎ 033 267 7243
🌐 www.cleomountain.com

Congella United National Breweries Ltd
21 Glastonbury Pl, Congella, Durban ☎ 031 205 5311

Copper Chimney
100 Denis Hurley St (former Queen St), Central Durban
☎ 031 306 0958/6223

Dargle Valley Pork
Dargle, Midlands ☎ 033 2344159

Gordon Road Fresh Food Market
40 Gladys Mazibuko Rd (former Marriott Rd), Greyville, Durban

Granny Mouse Country House
R103 near Lidgetton, Midlands
☎ 033 234 4071
🌐 www.grannymouse.co.za

The Grapevine
74 Main St, Howick
☎ 033 330 4556

Günther's
Caversham Cottage, Caversham Valley, Midlands ☎ 033 234 4171

Hartford House
Hlatikulu Rd, Mooi River, Midlands
☎ 033 263 2713
🌐 www.hartford.co.za

Horizons Gourmet Picnics
D146 off R103, Rosetta, Midlands
☎ 033 267 7027 or 082 895 1042
🌐 www.horizonsgourmet.co.za

Ijuba-United National Breweries Ltd
Dundee ☎ 031 205 5311

Ile Maurice
9 McCausland Cres, uMhlanga Rocks ☎ 031 561 7606

Indian Summer
Sunningdale Centre, uMhlanga Rocks Dr, Sunningdale, Durban North ☎ 031 562 1234

Jewel of India
Southern Sun Elangeni, 63 Snell Parade, North Beach ☎ 031 337 8168
🌐 www.jewelofindia.co.za

Karkloof Market
Off Karkoof Rd, Howick, Midlands
☎ 082 820 8986 or 082 851 8649

Little India
55 Musgrave Rd, Berea, Durban
☎ 031 201 1121

Little Poland Restaurant and Pub
38 Hilton Ave, Hilton, Midlands
☎ 033 343 4289
🌐 www.littlepoland.co.za

Mad About Cows
The Faraway Tree (former Hobbit's Hut), Boddington Farm, off R103 between Nottingham Road and Rosetta, Midlands ☎ 033 266 6833
🌐 www.ballina.co.za

Marrakesh Cheese Farm
R103, Rosetta, Midlands
☎ 033 267 7258

Nottingham Road Brewery
Rawdons Estate, Nottingham Road, Midlands ☎ 033 266 6728
🌐 www.rawdons.co.za

CONTACT DETAILS

Palki
225 Musgrave Rd, Berea, Durban
☎ 031 201 0019

Peel's Honey Shop
Exit 99 from the N3, Howick South, Underberg ☎ 033 330 3762

Pietermaritzburg Farmers' Market
Alexandra Park, Princess Elizabeth Dr ☎ 083 653 5848
www.pmbfarmersmarket.co.za

Roma Revolving Restaurant
32nd floor, John Ross House, Esplanade, Margaret Mncadi Ave (former Victoria Embankment), Durban ☎ 031 337 6707
www.roma.co.za

Rotunda Farm Stall
1 Cedara Rd, Hilton, Midlands
☎ 033 343 4205

Shongweni Brewery
Hillcrest, Durban ☎ 031 769 2061

Shongweni Farmers' Market
Cnr Kassier and Alverstone Rds, Assagay ☎ 083 777 1674
www.shongwenimarket.co.za

South African Breweries Ltd
9–25 Jeffels Rd, Prospecton West
☎ 031 910 111

Spice
362 Lilian Ngoyi Rd (former Windermere Rd), Morningside, Durban ☎ 031 303 6375

The Stables Wine Estate
Nottingham Road, Midlands
☎ 033 266 6781
www.stableswine.co.za

Swissland Cheese
Balgowan, Midlands
☎ 033 234 4042

Taj Mahal
Durban North ☎ 031 563 0533

Umami
1 Salt Rock Rd, Salt Rock
☎ 032 525 4615
www.umami.co.za

Ulundi Restaurant
Royal Hotel, 267 Anton Lembede St (former Smith St), Durban
☎ 031 333 6000
www.theroyal.co.za

Victoria Street Market
151 Bertha Mkhize St (former Victoria St), Durban
☎ 031 306 4021

The Waffle House
839 Marine Dr, Ramsgate, Margate
☎ 039 314 9424

Early Morning Market
100 Julius Nyerere Ave (former Warwick Ave), Durban

The Whistling Duck
Gowrie Ave, Nottingham Road, Midlands ☎ 033 266 6346

The Wine Cellar
Old Main Rd (R103) Rosetta, Midlands ☎ 033 267 7044
www.thewinecellar.co.za

Zimbali Lodge
☎ 031 762 2050
www.zimbali.org

Zululand Brewing Company
eShowe ☎ 035 474 4919

BEACH AND SEA

Aliwal Shoal
uMkomaas ☎ 039 973 2534
www.aliwalshoal.com

Beach Café
Bay of Plenty, Durban
☎ 031 332 8302
www.beachcafe.co.za

Cargo Hold
uShaka Marine World,
1 Bell St, Durban
☎ 031 328 8065
www.ushakamarineworld.co.za

Cool Runnings Fishing Charters
49 Milne St, Durban
☎ 031 368 5604 or 084 701 6912
www.coolrunnings.co.za

Coral Divers
Sodwana Bay
☎ Reservations 033 345 6531
☎ Resort 035 571 0290
www.coraldivers.co.za

The Deck
139 Lower OR Tambo Parade (former Lower Marine Parade), Durban
☎ 031 368 3699

Hakuna Matata Charters
Durban Marina, off Margaret Mncadi Ave (former Victoria Embankment), Durban
☎ 031 307 3782
www.hmcharters.co.za

iSimangaliso Wetland Park
North Coast ☎ 035 590 1633
www.isimangaliso.com

Joe Cool's
Durban Beachfront ☎ 031 332 9697
www.joecools.co.za

KZN Sharks Board
1a Herrwood Dr, uMmhlanga
☎ 031 566 0400
www.shark.co.za

Lifeguards
☎ 084 449 9964
lifeguardsafrica@hotorange.co.za

Lynski
Durban
☎ 031 539 3338 or 082 445 66 00
www.lynski.com

MacNicol's Bazley Beach Caravan & Camping Resort
Bazley Beach, South Coast
☎ 039 977 8863
www.macnicol.co.za

Minitown
OR Tambo Parade (former Marine Parade), North Beach, Durban
☎ 031 337 7892

Moyo uShaka Pier
uShaka Marine World, 1 Bell St, Durban ☎ 031 332 0606
www.ushakamarineworld.co.za

Mtunzini Country Club
Hely Hutchinson Rd, Mtunzini
☎ 035 340 1188

Oceanographic Research Institute
Durban ☎ 031 328 8222
www.ori.org.za

Pumula Beach Hotel
Off N2 South, uMzumbe, South Coast ☎ 039 684 6717
www.pumulabeachhotel.com

Rachel Finlayson Pool
133 Lower OR Tambo Parade (former Lower Marine Parade), North Beach, Durban
☎ 031 335 3712

Rocktail Beach Camp and Lodge
Rocktail Bay, iSimangaliso Wetland Park ☎ 011 257 5111
www.rocktailbay.com

San Lameer
Off N2 near Margate, South Coast
☎ 039 313 5141
☎ Villa rentals 039 313 0450
www.sanlameer.co.za

Suncoast Casino & Entertainment World
Suncoast Boulevard, OR Tambo Parade (former Marine Parade), Durban ☎ 031 328 3000
www.suncoastcasino.co.za

Southern African Sustainable Seafood Initiative (SASSI)
☎ 021 421 9167
☎ FishMS 079 499 8795
www.wwfsassi.co.za

Trafalgar Marine Reserve
☎ Contact Ezemvelo KZN Wildlife

uMdoni Park Golf Course Club
Minerva Rd, Pennington
☎ 039 975 1615
www.umdonipark.com

uShaka Marine World
1 Bell St, Durban ☎ 031 328 8000
www.ushakamarineworld.co.za

Wilson's Wharf
Durban   www.wilsonswharf.co.za

GAME AND NATURE PARKS

Bayete Zulu Game Lodge
Zululand Rhino Reserve, P450 off N2 North, near Hluhluwe
☎ 035 595 8089
www.bayetezulu.co.za

Beachwood Mangrove Nature Reserve
Off Riverside Rd, Durban North
☎ Contact Ezemvelo KZN Wildlife

Dlangala Wildlife Sanctuary
52 Margaret St, iXopo
☎ 039 834 2111

Durban Botanic Gardens
Cnr Botanic Gardens and St Thomas Rds, Berea, Durban
☎ 031 309 1170 or 031 201 1303
www.durbanbotanicgardens.org.za

CONTACT DETAILS

Enseleni Nature Reserve
11 km north of eMpangeni on the N2 ☎ 082 559 2852 or contact Ezemvelo KZN Wildlife

Entumeni Nature Reserve
20 km from eShowe on the Nkandla Rd
☎ Contact Ezemvelo KZN Wildlife

Giba Gorge
110 Stockville Rd Westmead, Durban ☎ 031 769 1527
🌐 www.gibagorge.co.za

Harold Johnson Nature Reserve
North Coast, 100 km from Durban
☎ 032 486 1574

iSimangaliso Wetland Park
North Coast ☎ 035 590 1633
🌐 www.isimangaliso.com

Karkloof Conservation and Tourism Centre
Howick, Midlands ☎ 033 330 2992
🌐 www.karkloofconservation.org.za

Kenneth Stainbank Nature Reserve
90 Coedmore Rd, Yellowwood Park, Durban ☎ 031 469 2807

KZN National Botanical Garden
2 Swartkops Rd, Prestbury, Pietermaritzburg ☎ 033 344 3585

Leopard Mountain Game Lodge
Zululand Rhino Reserve, off N2 North, between Hluhluwe and Mkhuze ☎ 035 595 8218
🌐 www.leopardmountain.co.za

Makaranga Garden Lodge
1A Igwababa Rd, Kloof, Durban
☎ 031 764 6616
🌐 www.africanpridehotels.com

Mount Currie
Southern Drakensberg, 6 km from Kokstad ☎ 039 727 3844

Mount Moreland Wetlands
Lake Victoria Conservancy, Charles St, Mount Moreland, near uMdloti
☎ 031 568 1557/1671

Mpenjati Nature Reserve
20 km south of Margate
☎ 039 313 0531

Msinsi Holdings
43 Old Main Rd, Hillcrest, Durban
☎ 031 765 7724

Oribi Gorge Nature Reserve
21 km from Port Shepstone
☎ 039 679 1644

Phinda Private Game Reserve
Off N2 North, near Hluhluwe
☎ 011 809 4300
🌐 www.phinda.com

Phongolo Nature Reserve
40 km from Mkhuze on the Golel Rd ☎ 034 435 1012

Rhino River Lodge
Zululand Rhino Reserve, P450 off N2 North ☎ 083 781 4924
🌐 www.rhinoriverlodge.co.za

South African National Biodiversity Institute (SANBI)
☎ 011 2843 5000
🌐 www.sanbi.org

Skyline Nature Reserve
Between uVongo and Margate
☎ 039 315 0112

Tembe Elephant Park
72 km from Jozini
☎ 031 267 0144
🌐 www.tembe.co.za

Thanda Private Game Reserve
D242, off N2, near Hluhluwe
☎ 011 469 5082/3/4/5
🌐 www.thanda.com

uMhlanga Lagoon Nature Reserve
Adjacent to Breakers Hotel, Lagoon Dr, uMhlanga Rocks
☎ 031 561 4257

uMlalazi Nature Reserve
2 km south of Mtunzini
☎ 035 340 1836/9

Umtamvuna Nature Reserve
iZingolweni Rd, Port Edward
☎ 039 311 2383

Vernon Crookes Nature Reserve
10 km from uMzinto
☎ 039 974 2222

Wagendrift Dam and Nature Reserve
6 km from Estcourt
☎ 036 352 5520

Weenen Game Reserve
10 km from Weenen
☎ 036 354 7013

Wildlife and Environment Society of South Africa (WESSA)
100 Brand Rd, Durban
☎ 031 201 3126
🌐 www.wildlifesociety.org.za

Zululand Rhino Reserve
Zululand Rhino Reserve, P450 off N2 North, near Hluhlwe
🌐 www.zululandrhinoreserve.co.za

WORLD HERITAGE WETLAND

iSimangaliso Wetland Park
North Coast ☎ 035 590 1633
🌐 www.isimangaliso.com

Wildlands Conservation Trust
☎ 033 343 6380
🌐 www.wildlands.co.za

Cape Vidal
35 km from St Lucia Village
☎ 035 590 9012/05

Mabibi Coastal Camp
Lake Sibaya ☎ 035 574 8998

False Bay Park
16 km from Hluhluwe Village
☎ 035 562 0425

Maphelane
Mfolozi River Mouth, south bank Mfolozi River ☎ 035 590 1407

Rocktail Beach Camp and Lodge
Rocktail Bay
☎ 011 257 5111
🌐 www.rocktailbay.com

St Lucia Crocodile Centre
St Lucia ☎ 035 590 1777

Thonga Beach Lodge
Thonga Beach Lodge, Mabibi/Lake Sibaya ☎ 035 474 1473

uMkhuze
28 km from Mkuze Village
☎ 035 573 9004/1

Fanie's Island
16 km from Hluhluwe Village
☎ 035 550 9000/02/35

WORLD HERITAGE MOUNTAINS

Cathedral Peak
☎ 036 488 1880

Cobham
☎ 033 702 0831

Drakensberg Boys' Choir
Winterton
☎ 036 468 1012
🌐 www.dbchoir.info

Falcon Ridge Birds of Prey Display Centre
☎ 082 774 6398

Garden Castle
☎ 033 701 1823

Giant's Castle
65 km from Estcourt
☎ 036 353 3718

Highmoor
☎ 033 267 7240

Himeville
☎ 033 702 1036

Injisuthi
☎ 036 431 7848

Kamberg
☎ 033 267 7251

Lammergeier Private Nature Reserve
☎ 036 353 3718

Lotheni
☎ 033 702 0540

Mkhomazi
☎ 033 2666 444

Royal Natal (Mahai & Rugged Glen)
45 km from Bergville
☎ 036 438 6310

Royal Natal (Thendele)
45 km from Bergville
☎ 036 438 6411

Sani Top Chalet
☎ 033 702 1069
🌐 www.sanitopchalet.co.za

Thokozisa Lifestyle Centre
10 km from Winterton on the R600
☎ 036 488184

uKhahlamba-Drakensberg Park
Drakensberg
☎ 033 239 1500 or contact Ezemvelo KZN Wildlife

Vergelegen
35 km from Himeville
☎ 033 702 0712

CHEVIOT COURT

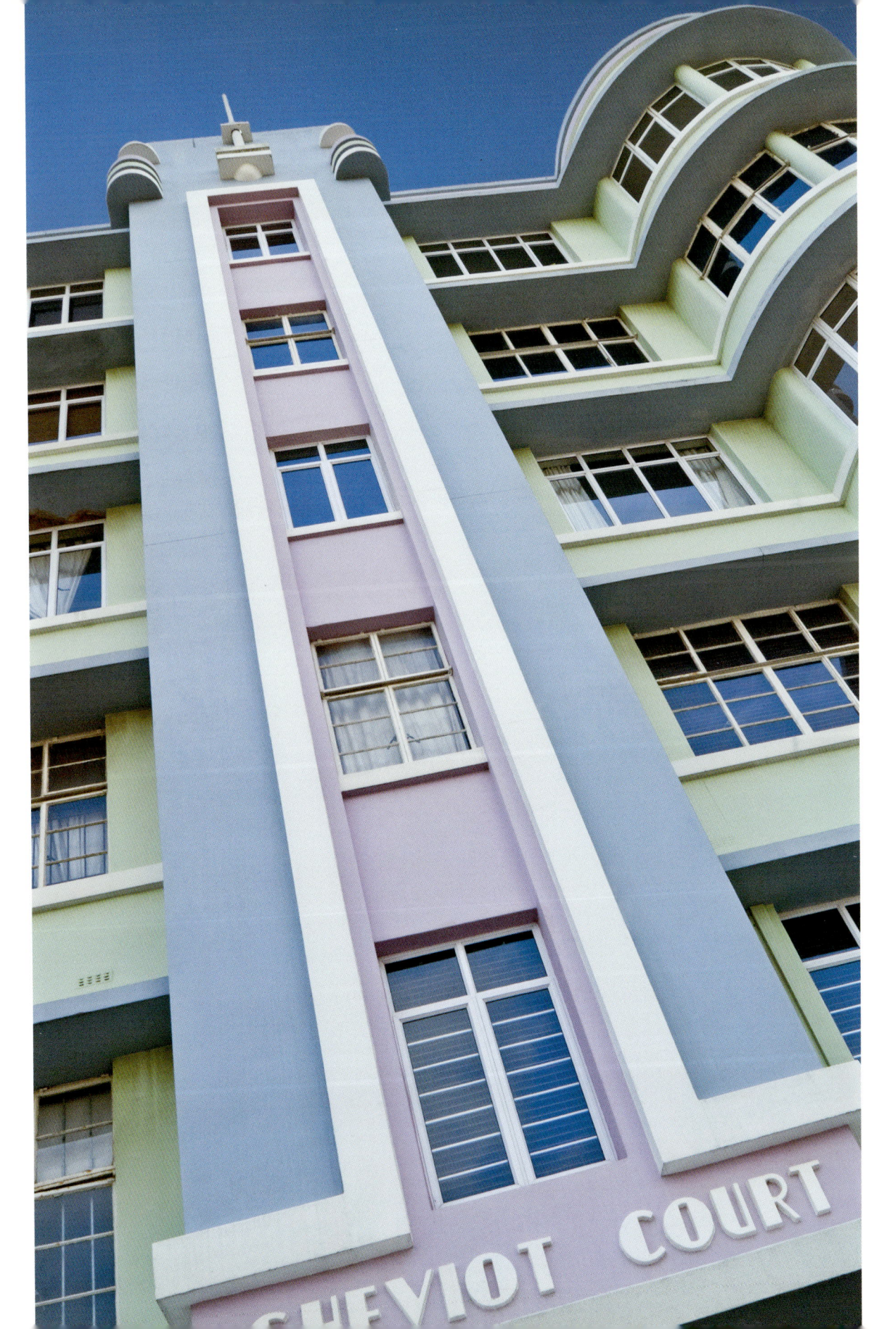

INDEX

*Page numbers in **bold** indicate photographs*

A

abaThwa 15
activities 80–1. *See also* races and events
  abseiling 10, 58
  adventure sports 10, 56–9
  Jeep uShaka Surf and Adventure Centre 57
  JNC Helicopter Tours 59
  Karkloof Canopy Tours **58**
  whitewater rafting 57
Aerial Boardwalk, Dlinza Forest 95
Africa Centre for Health and Population Studies 42
Africana Collections, Killie Campbell 22
African Art Centre, The 43
African fish-eagle **115**
African traditional beliefs 26
agama, southern tree **105**
Air Safaris 59
alcohol 68–71
Aliwal Shoal 56, 82, 83
  Marine Protected Area 85
amadlozi 26
Amashovashova road cycle race 53
amathongo 26
Amphitheatre **120**, **127**
Amphitheatre Gardens, Durban 77
Aquatic Championships, South African Senior National 54
archaeological sites 106
architectur(e) 40–2
  -al features, Hindu temple **34**
  colonial **41**
  contemporary 42
  historic 40
  religious 41
Ardmore Ceramic Art studio, Caversham **44**
Art Deco buildings **39**, 42
art galleries 42–3
Art in the Park 42
arts and crafts 43–6, 130
artSPACE 43
arts, visual 42–6
Ayurvedic treatments 36

B

Ballito **77**
Barboure, William B 39, 40
barn swallows 98
Barnyard Theatres, The 46
Bashpaswedana 36
baskets, waterproof **42**
BAT Centre **43**
Bat's Cave 78
Battle Cave at Injisuthi 125
battle sites 10–1
  Blood River/Ncome 23
  Isandlwana **23**
  Talana, reenactment **22**
Bauchop Custom Knives and Swords 46
Baynesfield Estate 22
Beach and Bush (tours) 59
beaches 74–9
  Addington 77
  Battery 77
  Bay of Plenty 77
  Bazley 75
  Cape Vidal **78**
  Clarke Bay 78
  Dairy 77
  eThekwini 77
  Hibberdene 75
  Island Rock Beach 79
  Lala Nek 79
  Leisure Bay 74
  Margate 74
  Marina Beach 74
  New Beach 77
  North Beach 77
  Pennington 75
  Ramsgate 74
  Salmon Bay 78
  San Lameer 74
  Scottburgh Main Beach, South Beach 75
  Sea Park 75
  Sheffield Beach 78
  Shelley Beach 85
  Snake Park 77
  South Beach 77
  Southbroom **74**
  Southport 75
  St Michael's-on-Sea 75
  Suncoast Beach 77
  Thompson's Bay 78
  Trafalgar 74
  Treasure 89
  uMdloti 78
  uMhlanga 77
  uMtentwini 75

beaches cont.
  uMzumbe 75
  uShaka 76
  Willards 78
  Zinkwazi 78
beadwork **16**
  Amandla Beadwork 46
Bean Green coffee **65**
Beatrice Street YMCA 49
besintu 69
Biodiversity Institute, South African National 97
biological features
  iSimangaliso Wetland Park 102
  uKhahlamba-Drakensberg Park 120–1
birds 102
Black Mfolozi River **87**
Blue Lagoon 77
boat tours, deep sea 114
boat trips, St Lucia Lake 114
Botanical Garden, Pietermaritzburg 97, **98**
Botanic Gardens, Durban 97
breweries
  Congella United National Breweries Ltd 71
  Ijuba United National Breweries Ltd 71
  micro 71
  Nottingham Road Brewery **64**, 71
  SAB Miller 71
  Shongweni Brewery 71
  Shongweni Brewery's Robson's **70**
  South African Breweries Ltd 71
  Zululand Brewing Company 71
Brew Route 71
Buddhist Retreat Centre, iXopo **37**
Buffalo River **10–1**
building methods **40**
bunny chow **62**, 63
butterflies 102

C

Camp's Drift Weir **52**
canoe trail **114**
canopy tours **58**
Cape Vidal 111, **112**
  beach **78**
Casino, Suncoast – & Entertainment World 77
Catalina Theatre 46
Cathedral Peak **122–3**, 125

Didima Camp 125, **126**
  guided walks to rock art shelters 14
  Trail 132
caves 131
Centekow Mission 32
chaat 63
Champagne Valley 48
Cheese Farm, Marrakesh 66, **67**
Cheese, Swissland 65
Christians 31–3
Christmas Bay 78
Church of the Vow 33
City Hall, Pietermaritzburg **41**
clay pot, traditional **45**
cloisters, Mariannhill Monastery **33**
coastline, aerial view **59**
coelacanths 106–7
colonial architecture **41**
colonial buildings, red-brick 40
commercial harbours 81
Comrades Marathon 52
conservation efforts 89–90
Consumers' Species List 80
Cool Runnings 19, 56
  Fishing Charters 81
coral reefs 104
country clubs
  Mtunzini 78
  San Lameer 55
  Selbourne 55
  Wild Coast Sun 55
Craft Shop, Hillcrest Aids Centre & 46
Crafts initiative, Wetland 45
Craft Village, 1000 Hills 46
Craft Village, Umnini 45
cricket 56
Crocodile Centre, St Lucia 114
crocodile hatchling **101**
Cultural Centre, Emnambithi 19
cultural tourism
  iSimangaliso 108, 108–11
cultural village 15–7, **17**
curry 62–3
Cyclone Extreme Products 57

D

da Gama, Vasco 11
dance 17, 48–9, **49**
  annual Royal Reed 18, 19
  Fantastic Flying Fish Dance Company 48
  Flatfoot Dance Company 48
  gumboot **48**

INDEX

dance cont.
    Hindu temple **13**
    Nateshwar Dance Academy 48
    Phenduka Dance Theatre 48
    Siwela Sonke Dance Theatre 48
Diamond Jubilee Pavilion 41
diving **56**, 114
    Coral Divers 84
    scuba 114
    with sharks **73**
Dlinza 95
    Forest Aerial Boardwalk, eShowe **95**, 99
Dockyard Supper Theatre 46
dolphins **82**, 104
dragonflies 102
Drakensberg
    Boys' Choir **48**, 130
    Canopy Tour **58**
    Central **122–3**
    places to stay 125
    San 15
    Southern **133**
    things to do 130
Dube, John 19
    Grave 18
Dundee 71
    Police Station 20
dunes, vegetated **106**
Durban 20, 75–7
    Art Deco Society 42
    Art Gallery 42
    Country Club 55
    Cultural and Documentation Centre 20
    harbour mouth **80**
    Jewish Club 31
    July 54
    Port of 81
    University of Technology Gallery 43
Dusi Canoe Marathon **52**

E

eateries
    Aubergine & Andreotti's 63
    Banana Café and Pancake House 64
    Britannia Hotel 62
    Café 1999 63
    Café Bloom 66
    Cafe Vacca Matta 47
    Cargo Hold 76
    Caversham Mill Restaurant 65

eateries cont.
    Cleopatra Mountain Farmhouse 67
    Copper Chimney 62
    Dargle Valley Pork 66
    Eden on Essenwood 47
    Granny Mouse Country House & Spa 65
    Günther's 65
    Hartford House 67
    Horizons Gourmet Picnics 66
    Ile Maurice 63
    Indian Summer 63
    Jewel of India 62
    Joe Cool's 56, 77
    Little India 62
    Little Poland Restaurant and Pub 71
    Mo's 63
    Moyo uShaka Pier 76
    Palki 62
    Rainbow Restaurant 47
    Roma Revolving Restaurant 63
    Spice 63
    Taj Mahal 63
    The Deck 77
    The Grapevine deli 65
    The Waffle House 64
    The Whistling Duck 66
    The Wine Cellar 66
    Thunder Road Rock Diner 47
    Ulundi, Royal Hotel 62
    Umami at Ballito 64
    Yossi's Café 47
    Zimbali Lodge 64
elephant **93**
    reintroductions 107
Elephant Park, Tembe 92
Elizabeth Sneddon Theatre 46
Emnambithi Cultural Centre 19
Entumeni 95
eShowe 71, 99
Ethnology, Mashu Museum of 22
European culture 21–2
Ezemvelo KZN Wildlife 74, 83, 89, 90, 107, 111, 120
    major reserves 90–2

F

Falcon Ridge Birds of Prey Display Centre 130
False Bay Park 112
Fanie's Island 112
Fardoun Spa 59

farmers' market
    Shongweni 67
    Karkloof 68
    Pietermaritzburg 68
    Shongweni 67
festivals
    Diwali, the Festival of Lights 36
    Janmastami Festival 36
festivals and ceremonies 21
    Diwali, the Festival of Lights 36
    Festival of Chariots 36
    Holi, the Festival of Colours 36
    Porridge Festival 34
    Ratha Yatra Festival 36
    Shembe 26–8
    Shembe and Zionists 28
    Snake Ceremony 28
    Splashy Fen 48
fever trees **9**, **94–5**
fires 132
fish-eagle, African **115**
fishing 58, 81
    Charters, Cool Runnings 81
    off the piers, Margate **80**
fish traps, ancient **110**, 111
flowering plants 102
fly-fishing 133
flying 59
fonya, traditional 110–1
    basket **111**
football 56
fossils 106
fresh food markets 67–8
frog species 104
Fugitives Drift **10–1**
    Lodge **23**

G

Gaboon adder **104**
game drives 114
Game Pass Shelter, Kamberg **14**, 125
game reserves
    Ithala 92
    Ndumo **9**, 92, **94–5**
    Phinda Private 94
    private 92–4
    Thanda Private 94
    Weenen 92
Gandhi, Mahatma 20, 21, 23, 26
    Phoenix settlement 18, 20
    statue **21**
Garden Castle 128
Garden of Remembrance 31
gardens 97–8

Giant's Castle **117**, 125, **128**, **130**
    Camp 128
    guided walks to rock art shelters 14
    Main Caves 125
    MTB Challenge 53
Giant's Cup 131
    Hiking Trail 128
Giba Gorge 95
golf 55. *See also* country clubs
    Beachwood golf course 55
    Prince's Grant 55
    Southbroom Golf Course **55**
    uMdoni Park Golf Course Club 75
Gorge swinging **58**
Grill Room, Oyster Box Hotel **63**
guided walks 114
    rock art 14
gumboot dancing **48**, 49
Gunston 500 79

H

Hakuna Matata Charters 81
Hare Krishnas 36
Hazrath Soofie Saheb Masjid **29**
Helicopter Services, South Coast 59
herbal medicines **18**
Hexagon Theatre 46
Highmoor 97
hiking
    Hiking Trail, Giant's Cup 128
    Lotheni mountain trails 119
    paths 131–2
    Primitive Trail 91
Hillcrest Aids Centre & Craft Shop 46
Hilltop Camp 91
Hilton Farm Stall 64, **66**
Himeville 97
Hindu 33–6
    deity Lord Muruga 20
    temple 20
    temple architectural features **34**
    temple dancers **13**
    Thirukootam and Sri Ganaser Temple 41
hippo **79**, **108**
Hlabisa, Zululand 42
Hluhluwe-iMfolozi Park **87**, 89, 90, 90–2
    iMfolozi section **97**
Holocaust Centre **31**
horse safaris 114
Hostel, KwaDabeka 18

INDEX

I
ice-cream farm, Mad About Cows 66
ilala palm wine 69–71
iMfolozi
  Base Camp Trail 91
  Big 5 MTB Challenge 53
  Wilderness Area **91**
  Wilderness Trails 91
iNcema 110
Indians 19–21
indlamu 49
ingoma 49
Injisuthi 125, 126
  guided walks to rock art shelters 14
Isandlwana **23**
  Lodge 23
  memorial 22
iSicathamiya 49
iSimangaliso
  cultural tourism 108
  Malaria programme 105
  places to stay 111
iSimangaliso Wetland Park 78, **79**, 82, 94
  Authority 89, 102, 107
  biological features 102
izindlu **40**
izithunzi 26

J
Jazz and Popular Music, The Centre for 47
Jews 30–1
Jo Thorpe Collection 22
Jummah Mosque **30**

K
Kamberg **14**, 125
  guided walks to rock art shelters 14
  Nature Reserve 128
  Rock Art Centre 125
Karkloof
  Canopy Tours **58**
  Classic Marathon 53
  Classic Mountain Bike Festival 53
  Conservation and Tourism Centre, Howick 97
  Spa Wellness & Wildlife Retreat 59
Kayak Safaris, St Lucia 57
Khekhekhe Mthethwa 28

Killie Campbell Museum 21
Kings Park Sporting Precinct 54
kiteboarding **57**, 80–1
Knives and Swords, Bauchop Custom 46
Kosi Bay 79, **110**, 112, **114**
  mouth **109**
kudu **106–7**
KwaDabeka Hostel 18
KwaZulu-Natal Society of Arts 43
KZN
  11 districts (municipalities) 11
  fact file 11
  list of major cities and towns 11
  National Botanical Garden, Pietermaritzburg 97
  origins of name 11
KZNSA 43

L
Ladysmith Black Mambazo choir 19
Lake Sibaya 113
La Mercy Lagoon **57**
leatherback turtles **84**
Library, Killie Campbell Africana 22
lifeguards 74
lilies **101**
lodges
  Bayete Zulu Game Lodge 90
  DumaZulu – & Traditional Village 17
  Fugitives Drift 23
  Isandlwana 23
  Kosi Forest **59**
  Leopard Mountain Game 90
  Makaranga Garden 98
  Rhino River 90
  SpionKop 23
  Thonga Beach 113
  Zimbali 64
Lotheni 128
  mountain trails **119**
Lourdes Mission 32
Lubombo Transfrontier Conservation and Resource Area 104
Lynski 81

M
Mabibi Coastal Camp 113
malaria 95
  programme, iSimangaliso 105

Maloti-Drakensberg Transfrontier and Conservation Project 118
managing the wilds 89
mangroves **103**
  tree species 104
Maphelane 112
Maputaland 84
  coast 103
  Sea Turtle Monitoring and Protection Programme 84
Margate **75**
  fishing off the pier **80**
Mariannhill Monastery 32, **33**
Maria Ratschitz Mission 32
Mariathal Mission 32
marine environment 82–5
Marine Reserve, Trafalgar 74, 82
markets. *See also* farmers' markets
  Early Morning Market 68
  Gordon Road Fresh Food Market 68
  Muti Market 17–8
  Victoria Street Fish Market 68
microlighting 59
Midlands Meander 64
Midmar Mile 54
Minitown 77
Mission Rocks 78
Monk's Cowl 126
Mont-Aux-Sources 132
mosque **30**
mountain biking **53**, 58
Mountaineering, Peak High 58
Mount Currie 97
Mount Moreland Wetlands 98
Mpila Camp 91, **97**
Mr Price Pro 54, 79
Msinsi Holdings 89
Msunduzi River **52**
Mtamvuna River Gorge **96**
Mtunzini 78
Muckleneuk 22
mudhoppers, African **105**
Museum
  Killie Campbell 21
  Mashu – of Ethnology 22
  Voortrekker/Msunduzi Museum 40
music 46–8
Muslim 28–30
  community **30**
  woman **20**
Muti Market 17–8, **18**
Mziki Trail 113–4

N
nature reserves
  Beachwood Mangrove 95
  Enseleni 94
  Harold Johnson 94
  Kamberg 128
  Kenneth Stainbank 95
  Lammergeier Private 133
  Mpenjati 96
  Oribi Gorge 96
  Phongolo 94
  Skyline 96
  Umbogavango 89
  Umgeni Valley 89
  uMhlanga Lagoon 95
  uMlalazi 94
  Umtamvuna 96
  Vernon Crookes 95
  Wagendrift Dam 97
nature reserves and conservancies 94–7
Ndumo Game Reserve 92, **94–5**
  pans **9**
North Coast 77–9
Nottingham Road 66
Ntshondwe 92
Nyamithi Pan **94–5**

O
Oceanographic Research Institute 83
olives, Romesco Olives, Howick 64
Ondini Historical Complex 40
Oribi Gorge **58**
  Nature Reserve 96
Oyster Box Hotel, uMhlanga Rocks 63

P
padkos 64
palm wine (ilala) 69
Peel's Honey Shop 64
performing arts 46–8
Perrier's Rocks 78
Pfanner, Prior Franz 33
  statue **25**
Phantom Ship 76
Phoenix 20, 34. *See also* Gandhi
Pietermaritzburg
  City Hall **41**
  Farmers' Market 68
pilgrimage, Shembe 26–8
Playhouse Theatre Complex 46, **47**, 49
Ponto do Ouro–Kosi Bay Transfrontier Conservation Area 104

INDEX

Pool, Rachel Finlayson 77
Port Edward 46, 74, 96
potato bass **56**, **83**
Prins, Frans (anthropologist) 15
Prospecton West 71
protected areas 11
Pumula Beach Hotel 75

R
races and events 52–6
raffia palm plantation 78
Rainbow Gorge, Cathedral Peak **129**
rainfall 11
Rare, Threatened & Endemic Species Project 107–8
Rawdons Hotel 71
Rebellion of Langalibalele 23
Reed Dance, annual Royal 18, 19
reefs and diving 84–5
Resort, Champagne Sports 55
rhinoceros
   black **89**, 102
   Black Rhino Range Expansion Project 89–90
   Operation Rhino 89
   white **90**
   Zululand Rhino Reserve 90
Rhumbelow Theatre, The 46
Richards Bay, Port of 81
Richenau Mission 32
Riverside, Durban North 29
rock art **14**, **15**, **124–5**, 125. *See also* San
rock climbing 58
Rocktail Beach Camp 79, 113
Rorke's Drift 23
Rotunda, The 66
Royal Natal Park 125, **131**
   guided walks to rock art shelters 14
rugby 56

S
San 14
   culture, guided walks 14
   Drakensberg 15
   rock art **14**, **15**, **124–5**
sangomas **18**
Sani Pass 130, **133**
Sani Top Chalet 130
Sardine Run **83**
sea kayaking 80
sea turtles 85, 104
Shakaland 17
shale house 40

Sharks Board, KZN 83–4
Sharks, The (rugby team) 56
Shembe 26–8, 28
   community **27**
Shirodhara 36
ski boats 81
SkyCar 54
Skydive Durban 59
skydiving, Blue Sky 59
Skyguide Paragliding 59
snake species 104
Snehana 36
snorkelling 114
Sodwana Bay 56, 79, 83, 84, 113
South Coast 74–5
spas 59
   Granny Mouse Country House & Spa 65
   Karkloof Spa Wellness & Wildlife Retreat 59
   SanAquam Urban Ayurvedic Spa 36
spices, aromatic **62**
Spioenkop 23
Sri Ambalavanaar Alayam Temple 33
Sri Ganaser Temple 41
Sri Ganesha Temple 34
Sri Jagannath Puri Temple 34
Sri Mariamman Temple 36
Sri Muruga Kovil **20**
   architectural features **34**
Sri Sri Radhanath Temple of Understanding 36
   ceiling **35**
SS Nebo **82**
Stadium, Moses Mabhida **54**
stage production
   Lion of the East **49**
   My Fair Lady **46**
Star of David **31**
statues, Siddhārtha Gautama **37**
Stebel Rocks 75
St Lucia
   Crocodile Centre 114
   Estuary **79**
   Kayak Safaris 57
Sufi Mosque 41
Sufi Order, int. headquarters 29
surfing **51**, 57, 80
Surrey Mansions **39**
Sustainable Seafood Initiative, Southern African 80
Swimming World Cup 54
sycamore **9**

T
Tatham Art Gallery 42, **43**
temperatures 11
Terbodore Coffee Roasters, Curry's Post **67**
thali 62
theatre 46
Thendele Camp 126
Thokozisa Lifestyle Centre 130
township tour 18
traditional village
   PheZulu Safari Park 17
Traditional Village, DumaZulu Lodge & 17
Transfrontier Conservation Areas 104–6
tree frog **104**
Tsonga fishermen **111**
Tugela Falls 125, **127**
turtle breeding ritual 114
turtle tours 84
Twinstreams Education Centre 89

U
ubusulu 69
uKhahlamba-Drakensberg Park 14, 118–21, **122–3**, 127
   Amphitheatre 120–1
ukhamba pot **45**
uLundi 40
uMhlanga Rocks 63, **76**
uMkhuze 112
   tented camp **113**
uMkomaas 56
umqombothi 69, 71
uMvelinqangi 26
unique areas 102
Uprising, Bhambatha 23
uShaka
   Marine World 56, 76, 84
   Sea World 76
   Village Walk 76
   Wet 'n Wild 76
uThukela Gorge 132
utshwala 69

V
Vishnu Temple 41
visual arts 42–6
vulture, bearded 132, **133**
   restaurants 133

W
Wagendrift Dam and Nature Reserve 97
wattle-and-daub houses 40
Wave House 57
Wetland Crafts initiative 45
whales **85**, 104, 114
whale sharks 104
Wild 5 58
Wilderness Area, Mdedelelo 126
wilderness trail **91**
wild flowers, paper hearts **132**
Wildlands Conservation Trust 107
Wildlife and Environment Society of South Africa 89
Wildlife Sanctuary, Dlangala 96
William Campbell Furniture and Picture Collection 22
Wilson's Wharf 81
windsurfing and kiteboading 80–1
wine 68–9
Wine Cellar, The 66
Wine Estate, Abingdon, Lions River **69**
Wine Estate, The Stables 68–9
Wire Art, Israel's 46
woMhlanga 18
World Wide Fund For Nature South Africa 80, 90
Woza Moya Project 37

Z
Zero Four Flight School 59
Zimbali Country Club 55
Zionists 28
Zulu 15–9, 26
   beadwork **16**
   beer, home-brewed, traditional **65**, 69–70
   culture 15–7, **17**
   home-brewed beer **65**
   homestead **40**
   modern rural homestead **26**
   Traditional Village 17
   woman **16**
Zulu Jazz Lounge 47

Acknowledgements

Sue Derwent and Roger de la Harpe would like to thank the many, many people throughout KZN who assisted in making this book possible by generously offering time, information, accommodation, access and friendly ears. A special thank you goes to long-suffering editor Leah van Deventer, designer Catherine Coetzer, managing editor Roelien Theron and publisher Claudia Dos Santos of the Travel & Heritage team at Random House Struik.

First published in 2010 by Struik Travel & Heritage
(an imprint of Random House Struik (Pty) Ltd)
Company Reg. No. 1966/003153/07
80 McKenzie Street, Cape Town, 8001
PO Box 1144, Cape Town 8000, South Africa

Copyright © in published edition: Random House Struik 2010
Copyright © in text: Sue Derwent 2010
Copyright © in maps: Random House Struik, MapStudio 2010
Copyright © in photographs: Roger de la Harpe 2010, with the exception of: Front cover (top right), Walter Knirr/Images of Africa; p. 23, *Illustrated London News* July–December 1979, MuseuMAfrica/Images of Africa; p. 37 (left), courtesy of Buddhist Retreat Centre; p. 46, Val Adamson, courtesy of The Playhouse Company; p. 49, courtesy of The Playhouse Company; p. 51, Jonathan Reid/Images of Africa; p. 61, Dirk Pieters/Images of Africa; and p. 80, SASSI logo courtesy of The Southern African Sustainable Seafood Initiative (SASSI).

Front cover (top to bottom, left to right): Zulu beadwork; frangipanis; cooking spices; and male tree agama
Back cover (left to right): Sri Muruga Kovil in Phoenix, Durban; Zulu *indlu*, near Melmoth; The Bat Centre, Durban
Spine: uMhlanga Pier, uMhlanga
Half-title page: Zulu ricksha men, Durban
Title page: Durban skyline
Contents pages (left to right): African marsh-harrier catching fish and Drakensberg Escarpment from Mike's Pass
Contact details: Cheviot Court, Durban

Publisher: Claudia Dos Santos
Managing editor: Roelien Theron
Editor: Leah van Deventer
Project coordinator: Alana Bolligelo
Designer: Catherine Coetzer
Cartographer: Elaine Fick
Indexer: Anna Tanneberger
Proofreader: Sean Fraser

Reproduction by Hirt & Carter Cape (Pty) Ltd
Printed and bound by Tien Wah Press (Pte) Limited, Singapore

ISBN 978 1 77007 395 1
10 9 8 7 6 5 4 3 2 1

All rights reserved. No part of this publication may be reproduced, stored in a retrieval system or transmitted, in any form or by any means, electronic, mechanical, photocopying, recording or otherwise, without the prior written permission of the publishers and the copyright holder(s). While every effort has been made to ensure that the information in this book was correct at the time of going to press, some details might since have changed. The authors and publishers accept no responsibility for any consequences, loss, injury, damage or inconvenience sustained by any person using this book. Please email any comments or updates to: kznadventuresincultureandnature@randomstruik.co.za

More than 50 000 unique African images are available to purchase from our image bank at:
www.imagesofafrica.co.za